PEONY

Peony

The Best Varieties for Your Garden

DAVID C. MICHENER &
CAROL A. ADELMAN

Timber Press
Portland, Oregon

Front cover (clockwise from top left): 'Carnation Bouquet', 'Callie's
Memory', 'Coral Sunset', 'Rozella', 'Love Affair', 'Candy Heart'
Title page: Peonies in bloom at the Nichols Arboretum, University of Michigan

Photo credits appear on page 240.

Published in 2017 by Timber Press, Inc.
The Haseltine Building
133 S.W. Second Avenue, Suite 450
Portland, Oregon 97204-3527
timberpress.com

Printed in China
Text design by Hillary Caudle and James Forkner
Cover design by Anna Eshelman

ISBN 978-1-60469-520-5

Catalog records for this book are available from the Library of Congress and the British Library.

Dedicated to all peony hybridizers: past, present, and future

CONTENTS

ACKNOWLEDGMENTS

We thank our editorial team at Timber Press for shepherding the idea of this book to reality. The helpful suggestions, precise revisions, and skillful editing are all gratefully appreciated. We thank our many friends and peony lovers who submitted a visual richness of images for review, only some of which were able to be included. All are beautiful. Joanne Koptur critiqued and meticulously edited the draft manuscript; she clarified meaning while retaining our voices.

⟫ — ⟪

David, a relative late-comer to peonies-as-passion, thanks Bob Grese (director) and all the members of the Peony Advisory Board of the University of Michigan's Nichols Arboretum Peony Garden who have been patient with me as I have learned far more than can be relayed here: Carol Adelman, Lindsey D'Aoust, Harvey Buchite, Peggy Cornett, Don Hollingsworth, Jeff Jabco, Reiner (and Alexis) Jakubowski, Scott Kunst, Scott Parker, Donald R. Smith, and Jim Waddick.

Adrienne O'Brien and Carmen Leskoviansky are skilled horticulturists who have re-grounded me many times in reality, aided by a series of inquisitive summer interns, work-study students, and volunteers. The many peony enthusiasts, experts, breeders, and nursery owners met at meetings, as of the American Peony Society, have opened my eyes to the depth of experienced knowledge that is so openly shared, and the wide range of beauty that is within peonies. Carol Dickerman helped me see meaningful aspects of historical context. Nastassia Vlasova and her colleagues at the Central Botanical Garden Minsk of the National Academy of Sciences of Belarus have broadened my understanding of many of these peonies (as well as their own) and how they perform on other shores.

Our peers at sister gardens in the Plant Collections Network in Canada and the United States have helped me be more skilled in evaluating and appreciating peonies in public venues. Our Peony Initiative has far too many individuals who have generously supported our project to list here. I've tried to be inclusive in our web site.

In addition, my colleague Nan Sinton has talked through many points. Since this book has been written outside my university duties, most of all I thank my husband, Wil Strickland, who has endured the many hours where this book took priority over much else in our life, including our own peonies. My gratitude to all.

⟫ — ⟪

Carol also thanks all those above who assisted David and her in preparing this book and would like to especially acknowledge the late Allan Rogers for both his personal advice and inspiration as well as his book *Peonies* published by Timber Press in 1995. It has been called the bible of peonies.

Carsten Burkhardt has spent tireless hours creating www.paeo.de, an invaluable compilation of peony literature, photos, and information that has been of great benefit to the peony world.

Don Hollingsworth stands out as not only a hybridizer but also a true mentor as were the late Bill Seidl and Myron Bigger. Thanks to the American Peony Society for their many publications, flower shows, and annual gatherings of peony lovers. I also thank David Michener for inviting me to join him in creating this book. Thanks also to Mother Nature and God for the exquisite creation—the peony.

INTRODUCTION

*P*eonies are stunningly beautiful, easy to grow, relatively carefree, and adaptable to any garden style. They are a favorite flower everywhere they can be grown and for good reason: the heady fragrances and enchanting colors of a peony-rich garden can evoke memories, capture an enchanted moment, and represent hope, friendship, romance, or gracious hospitality.

Wherever winters are cold enough for peonies, gardeners have grown plants that have been shared with them or passed down among generations as treasured living family heirlooms. With their colors, fragrances, and forms, the cut flowers combine well in bouquets. Peonies simply have no rival in their season.

Peonies blossom in a wide variety of colors and shapes. Their color range encompasses every tint from pure white through myriad pinks to the deepest reds and rich, complex chocolate tones. Almost every shade is represented except for blue and black, though now some blossoms approach those shades, as with the dazzling deep lavenders of 'Lavender Hill' and 'Sonoma Amethyst'.

To add to the fun and depending on the cultivar, individual peony flowers may retain the same color from start to finish, or they may begin as one color and either fade or darken to another related color. Some selections are bicolored, and, more rarely seen, tricolored. Contemporary breeders are even providing gardeners with new striped peonies such as 'Candy Stripe'—truly distinctive treasures. The individual flower shapes, which are called forms, can be as simple as a wild rose or so petal-stuffed that it is hard to imagine how all the petals ever fit in the bud, with many variations in between.

A bouquet of peonies, or even a single stem, can enhance any occasion. For floral designers, these blossoms offer much variation in visual texture and form, with petal edges that can be smooth, ruffled, or notched. Petals can be arranged in many configurations, from a single row to a tightly packed multitude.

Peonies easily combine with accent flowers and foliage. Their long, strong stems provide stature and the huge petals easily define luxury. Peonies are frequently used as event flowers as they have an enduring vase life of seven to ten days from bud that can be controlled by heat and light. They are a popular favorite in wedding bouquets and have earned that honor not only for their luxurious sheen and huge size, but also for colors that blend harmoniously with any setting.

From the several thousand selections currently available, we've chosen nearly two hundred of the best plants for garden and vase. Our goal in this book is to provide the information you need to grow these magnificent peonies with confidence, to create stunning garden scenes, and to enjoy your peonies as cut flowers. Peonies can do so much in the garden and with such little effort on the gardener's part that they should be considered whenever a gardener wonders about what plant would best complement a particular spot.

Appreciating and understanding the differences between the three basic types of peonies adds to their versatility in garden compositions and is a big part of the fun of planting these flowers. The three plant types are commonly called bush, tree, and Itoh/intersectional. Each type has its own range of floral seasons and colors, as well as some specialized horticultural needs.

The most common type of peony is the herbaceous form, also called bush peony. Members of this group grow each year to the size of small shrubs, bloom in a complete range of whites to reds, and then die to the ground for the winter, resprouting the next spring.

Tree peonies are shrubs with distinctively thick woody stems that last for many years. They begin their bloom season earlier than the bush peonies, with the advantage that the flower color covers the same range as the herbaceous peonies and additionally brings in yellow, gold, lavender, and purple to nearly black.

The Itoh/intersectional peonies are hybrids between the bush and tree peonies. They were first developed in the mid-twentieth century and they combine the best attributes of both parents. New intersectional hybrids have fantastic colors and abundant floral displays along with the lovely foliage that flows into a pleasingly shaped shrub, making them increasingly popular.

We love all peonies!

The diverse colors and forms make these plants supremely useful for incorporating in all garden styles. Peonies are bold when massed in beds and borders, yet equally stately when integrated among other perennials and shrubs. Peonies are also stunning when used as accent notes in informal plantings. Their roles for garden designers extend well after their bloom season as a backdrop for bright garden colors. Perhaps uniquely among garden perennials, peonies contribute the lush green foliage to the essential summer verdancy that helps such later-blooming perennials as bee balms (*Monarda*), lilies (*Lilium*), gladiolus (*Gladiolus*), phlox (*Phlox*), and many others become colorful features of their season.

For gardeners with a keen color sense, the unheralded colors of peony sprouts as they emerge from the ground provide striking accent notes in spring display beds. Watch the distinctively colored sprouts, described as red asparagus, so you can plan the next year's color scheme for tulips and pansies.

Yellow and cream-colored peonies blend with purple iris, mauve dianthus, and salmon-colored lupines.

Yet another reason to revel in peonies is that deer and most other garden pests absolutely despise them. Only winter-starved mice and rabbits seem to have missed the message for tree peonies, but that's easily addressed with simple wire cages around the base of the plants during the winter. Insect pests are minimal, and foliage diseases mercifully few. Yes, there are ants on the flower buds, but they are a sign of a healthy garden.

If you're new to peonies, we think you'll soon be hooked for life, as are we. If you're already familiar with peonies, we want to share with you our selection of the best cultivars, from tried-and-true heritage forms to new favorites, and the unanticipated ways to incorporate them in your garden.

HOW TO USE THIS BOOK

Today's gardeners have an array of splendid peonies to choose from. Local garden centers offer a tempting selection, but to find many of the plants described here and scores more, you will need to shop among the mail-order and web-order peony sources and specialty growers listed at the end of this book. This broad palette of peonies makes it possible to find the right peonies for every garden, especially yours. In the gallery that follows, our intent is to guide gardeners and floral designers to find the peony selections that they like, appropriate for a wide range of styles, themes, and exhibition concepts.

The gallery highlights outstanding peonies that are commercially available in North America, although not necessarily carried by any one particular source. Our selections acknowledge current popularity; over one hundred of these entries are listed in at least three recent nursery catalogs or websites, or are recommended in contemporary publications and resources. The rest are ones we think are exceptional, even if not the most frequently offered or discussed. These, too, have been confirmed as available on the market and include new varieties that cannot be overlooked for their beauty and outstanding coloration.

There are far more peonies available and in gardens than could possibly be covered by a book several times the size of this one. Over four thousand named peony selections have been introduced into North American and Western Europe since the early nineteenth century with over half of those now believed to be lost to horticulture. It may come as a surprise that there are gardeners who have amassed personal peony collections with over five hundred choice cultivars, and some who have well over a thousand.

The peony descriptions are divided into three groups by plant form: bush, intersectional, and tree. Within each grouping, the plants are arranged alphabetically by name, regardless of the species or parentage.

Each entry has a consistent format accompanied by a photograph and includes the peony's name, the breeder, the country of origin, and the year the peony was introduced. Our opinion of a selection's best virtues follows, and as with people, some peonies take longer to extol than others, but brevity can also be an accolade. Think of a friend for whom "kind and reliable" would say it all; peonies are the same. When appropriate, shortcomings are noted here, which for some plants is the absence or degree of fragrance.

All the entries then list the category to which the selection belongs, followed by floral characteristics, including fundamental color(s), form, degree of fragrance, and season of main bloom (note that some tree peonies bloom before the herbaceous and hybrid forms). The height given is as known to us. Since peonies are living organisms, the listed heights by others, as found on the web and in catalogs, may differ slightly, but is usually within 3 inches (8 cm). This variation likely reflects growing conditions and plant maturity. Special notes on the selection's staking needs and value as cut flowers come next.

Where there's an interesting story or observation, historical significance and other notes are included. If any major awards offered by the American Peony Society (APS) at its annual Conference and Exhibition have been given, they are listed along with the Royal Horticultural Society's (RHS) Award of Garden Merit.

The historical notes should be especially helpful for gardeners seeking guidance on historic contexts. Since opinions of merit vary over time and some peonies have been popular for generations, the authoritative works (see Further Reading) of Alice Harding (1917) and Dr. William Upjohn (ca. 1923) are quoted. These two experts reflect different yet nearly contemporary perspectives from a critical era. In some cases, as with 'Edulis Superba', we find in their opinions that the more things change, the more they stay the same, even to our times.

Not all historic peonies listed in these two references are included. With continued hybridizing, improvement in flower and plant quality has given today's gardener many superior alternatives. Gardeners seeking to compare classic with contemporary peonies will want to visit a range of peony gardens, including the historic collections at the Nichols Arboretum or at Winterthur Garden

One of the best ways to see peonies in bloom and to compare the flowers is to attend a peony show hosted by the American or Canadian Peony Societies and their many local chapters. For understanding which peonies grow well in your area, visit the public gardens in your region that have large peony collections. To find these, consult the web resources of the American and Canadian Peony Societies, as well as the Peony Garden at the Nichols Arboretum. Remember that specialty peony nurseries may also have exemplary peony display gardens. Wherever you go, bring your copy of this book along and write your notes right in it.

Now to the fun: our parade of famous, favorite, and meritorious peonies. At least some of them need to be in your garden. Here's to the joy of peonies!

History

and

Origin

Where did all the beautiful peony varieties come from, and how does their ancestry guide us to grow them in our gardens?

Beauty from Nature

It may come as a surprise to imagine peonies as beautiful wildflowers, but most of the thirty-five to forty-five wild species are just that. Botanists haven't always agreed how many species and natural variations exist. Over the past two centuries they have described and named more than four hundred.

It is agreed that peonies are native from southern Europe, through the islands in and around the Mediterranean, across Asia Minor, the Himalayas, and then into China, Korea, Japan, and the Russian Far East. All the wild species are native either to climates with cool winters and sufficient summer rain to keep the foliage alive until fall, or to the mountainous areas in two regions with Mediterranean-type climates. These are the Mediterranean itself and parts of the western United States.

For all their geographic spread, peonies are rarely common in the wild and about half the species are very local and threatened with extinction. Perhaps surprisingly, given all the thousands of garden selections of peonies, only a few wild species are the ancestors of our garden beauties.

In light of this reality, it makes sense that garden peonies grow best in situations that mimic the climate, soil, and rainfall conditions of the species' original environments. All ancestral species of ornamental peonies share northern climates with cool to cold winters, centered on zones 3 to 7 in the USDA system.

Wild *Paeonia tenuifolia*
in southern Europe.

In all cases, the wild plants are found on mineral-rich soils where the drainage is superb. Most are native to open woodlands, prairielike areas, or rocky slopes without a dense forest canopy; thus, they should have sun at least three-quarters of the day, about six hours and preferably more. The exceptions include woodland to forest peonies of eastern Asia and the peonies of western North America's dry-climate regions.

From the Wild to Our Gardens

Our rich abundance of peony selections is a cultural treasury that has taken centuries to amass and is still in prolific development. As the peony in nature is single-petaled, ancient gardeners captured and bred any rare, multipetaled bloom because of its unusual appeal. Discovering these doubled flowers must have been a bit like finding the four-leaf clover that occasionally occurs among the more typical three-leaf clovers.

In Asia, the demanding eyes of ancient gardeners and patrons across centuries of Chinese and Japanese connoisseurs have deeply set the genetic coding for ornamental virtues of peony flowers. Of course, those eyes kept pace with changing aesthetics of their respective eras; however, peonies were first appreciated for their herbal (medicinal) qualities. They were also greatly cherished for their intoxicating aroma, and, especially in China, many-petaled flowers were strongly preferred over single-petaled blooms. Stems that held multiple flowers were prized.

As these exquisite and highly refined selections became known as live garden plants in Europe and North America by the early nineteenth century, they had an immediate and sensational impact. The shift from Asian aesthetics to include those of Western cultures transformed peonies as we now know them.

There are two surprising elements in the history of peony introduction to the West. The first is that Western gardeners developed more cultivars of herbaceous peonies than tree peonies, which is the opposite of their history in Asia, where tree peonies were preferred. The second is that herbaceous peonies were bred primarily to be exceptional cut flowers rather than ornamental garden plants. Selecting peonies primarily for their garden pleasure and ease of maintenance only became a driving factor with the rise of a middle-class with leisure time—increasingly important as the twentieth century advanced.

The wild species that is the parent of the vast majority of herbaceous peonies is *Paeonia lactiflora*, and it naturally has many flower buds on one stem, but Western florists preferred one large flower per stem. That is why so many of the older herbaceous selections need to be both disbudded (the side buds removed) and staked. Then, as now, such peonies are ideal for bridal events, ceremonial occasions, and joyous bouquets of sheer immersive beauty.

PEONY BEAUTY IN ASIAN TRADITIONS

In Chinese culture, tree peonies, called *mou dan* or *moutan*, hold the place of honor, while herbaceous peonies, or *shoa-yao*, were less important until recent times. Tree peonies were being domesticated in China at least two thousand years ago. They were, and remain, prized for their large, bold flowers, with selections ranging through white, reds, purplish reds (some seem almost black), and yellow. Reportedly, some colors were prized for their imperial associations. By the Song Dynasty (960–1270), scores of named forms were recognized, and the rarest were highly sought by collectors.

Tree peonies became known as the King of Flowers. Centers of tree peony culture formed around several cities, of which Luoyang and Heze are best known in the West. These cities have numerous peony gardens. Some, such as the Luoyang National Peony Garden, display over a thousand different kinds of tree peonies. Several other gardens have centuries-old tree peony specimens.

Across the generations, going to view tree peonies in their peak bloom has been a much-anticipated rite of spring. An essential part of their appeal in the Chinese aesthetic is their fleeting and sensuous beauty. The elevated status of tree peonies is also reflected by their presence in highly valued Chinese art forms as textiles, paintings, and poetry.

By contrast, the herbaceous peonies, although beautiful, lacked high social status. Even so, there were more than thirty herbaceous varieties listed by the late sixteenth century, and they have since become known as the Prime Minister of Flowers.

In addition to being beautiful, both kinds of peonies had, and retain, roles in traditional Chinese medicine. It is their roots that are used, not the flowers.

Tree peonies were introduced to Japan, likely as early as the Heian period (794–1185), and became known as *botan*. Since there are no native tree peonies in Japan, it is clear all the Japanese tree peony selections are based on ancestral Chinese ornamental forms. Over the centuries, the Japanese aesthetic became distinctive for restrained yet intense colors and, in some selections, relative simplicity of flower form as compared to Chinese forms.

In Japan, the herbaceous peonies were introduced as medicinal plants by 800 AD. By the seventeenth century, several score of named herbaceous peonies were recorded. A series bred by samurai in the eighteenth century is still known for its beauty.

The history of peonies in Korea is poorly known in the West, but based on Korean arts, peony roles were and remain important in the culture.

PEONY BEAUTY IN EUROPEAN AND AMERICAN TRADITIONS

The important native peony in parts of southern Europe and the Mediterranean is *Paeonia officinalis*. Its roots have been considered a vital medicinal component since ancient times.

The genus name honors the mythical Paeon, the healer of the ancient Greek gods. In the Christian era, with the rise of monastic orders and medicinal gardens, peonies moved from the European wilds to cloistered gardens. The relative unimportance of peonies as ornamental plants in the West is indicated by how infrequently peonies are featured in Western art or high-status domestic articles as textiles and ceramics, a situation that did not change until Asian peony selections arrived by the early nineteenth century.

A wild red peony, complete with a visiting butterfly, is in the flowery foreground of *The Little Garden of Paradise* (1410–1420), a painting by an unknown artist of the Virgin Mary and several saints gathered in a walled garden. During the Renaissance, the red-flowered European species *Paeonia mascula* is depicted from the garden of the prince-bishop of Eichstatt in 1613. This was the garden tended by the great apothecary and botanist Basilius Besler, and perhaps not coincidentally, the medicinal connection surfaces once again. In Italy, the following year the painter Giraolamo Pini included the same species in a study of perennial plants appropriate for distinguished individuals to know.

As a garden flower, the ascendency of peonies in Europe began by the early nineteenth century when novel herbaceous and tree peonies began arriving in increasing numbers from the Far East. Recent molecular evidence with colleagues in Belarus indicates these were the highly selected forms primarily from Chinese aesthetic traditions, which makes historical sense since Japan was closed to the West until 1864. It is important to note that these garden novelties were probably not anything like the wild ancestral species. It has often been too easy to mistake domesticated plants from other cultures as wild plants when they are brought to new shores.

These hardy and beautiful peonies became sensations, but only the herbaceous peony became widespread in breeding programs, perhaps because of its ease of propagation of new selections by root divisions. The herbaceous peony craze, and a long-running craze it was, began in French nurseries. Modeste Guerin was introducing varieties by 1835, while Charles Verdier had over fifty of his own varieties by the 1850s. Among the early French classics, and rightfully still popular for contemporary gardeners, are 'Edulis Superba' by Nicholas Lemon in 1824, 'Festiva Maxima' by Auguste Miellez in 1851, and 'Duchesse de Nemours' by Jacques Calot in 1856.

For nearly two centuries, 'Edulis Superba' has been favored for its abundant, fragrant flowers.

Introduced by Félix Crouse in 1885, 'Madame de Verneville' is grown for its fragrant, double flowers on strong stems.

In North America, peonies followed a similar trajectory to that in Europe, but with a peculiar time lag. Thomas Jefferson was growing the classic European *Paeonia officinalis* at Monticello by 1771. The pioneering American nurseryman Bernard McMahon of the Philadelphia region listed five kinds of peonies in 1806, and William Robert Prince, the great American nurseryman in Long Island, New York, had at least three kinds from China by 1828. However, none of these were American selections.

The first American selections did not appear until H. A. Terry in Iowa introduced many of his seedlings after 1856, as did John Richardson in Massachusetts after 1857. Sarah Pleas of Indiana is the earliest important American female peony breeder, and her cultivars were introduced after 1880. Many early American selections are lost, but among the classics once again available are Richardson's 'Milton Hill' of 1891 and Pleas's 'Jubilee' of 1908. Within several years of being introduced, 'Jubilee' even made *The New York Times*, and both 'Jubilee' and Mrs. Pleas are still celebrated with an annual peony festival in Van Wert, Ohio.

By the late nineteenth century, over a thousand new herbaceous peonies had been bred and named by European and American breeders, mostly based on Chinese cultivars of *Paeonia lactiflora*, and a period of significant confusion over which peony flower had which name was in full fury. The American Peony Society was founded in 1903 with its first meeting in Detroit, Michigan. One of its purposes was to bring order out of this chaos. It took decades to remedy the problem, and to help the situation several important public peony gardens were founded in that era. Of course, peony breeders kept introducing new selections, as they still do. The American Peony Society and its International Registrar work at keeping the names in order, thereby helping build a worldwide, diverse community of peony lovers.

Some of the great peony breeders of the first half of the twentieth century specifically sought additional wild peony species for their work to extend the bloom season, obtain richer, more modern colors, and provide stronger stems. The stronger stems reflected the need for the plants to perform well in gardens so that they did not need to be staked. A. M. Brand in Minnesota, Lyman Glasscock and Charles Klehm in Illinois, and Arthur P. Saunders in New York are a few of the important North American breeders. Of these, Saunders was by far the most innovative, using multiple species in his myriad crosses. He introduced hundreds of novel bush and tree peonies. By 1950, over ninety American and Canadian citizens were recorded in the American Peony Society registers as having bred and named at least one peony; of these, twenty were women.

Although gardeners have a richness of herbaceous and tree peony selections to choose from today, for more than a century the Holy Grail was a hybrid between the two kinds, which represent different groups, or sections, of peonies. There is no obvious genetic barrier between the sections. The anticipated advantage of the hybrids was spectacular new colors, perhaps even tones and combinations yet unknown. In this the intersectionals have not disappointed. Likely there was the hope that they would combine the best of both parents in vigor and foliage, too.

Undismayed by the complete failure of others, Mr. Itoh of Japan had diligently hand-pollinated flowers to attempt a successful cross, but as with all prior workers, had no success. Then, starting in 1948, out of reportedly more than two thousand crosses, he finally succeeded, with at least six seedlings vigorous enough to live. But, by a cruel twist of fate, Mr. Itoh died before his plants were old enough to bloom. Louis Smirnow of New York was allowed to name and introduce four. They were immediately popular, initially commanding hundreds of dollars per plant in the prices of that era.

Since then, many breeders have used the knowledge of the basis of this cross for their own breeding programs and an entirely new peony section, the Itoh hybrids or Itoh intersectionals, has been internationally acclaimed and recognized. Fortunately, the prices are now within range of every peony lover. 'Bartzella' and 'Garden Treasure' have been favorite yellows since their introduction in the mid-1980s and are destined to become classic peonies in the generations ahead.

As a group, the intersectional peonies are at the center of some of the most active work for new introductions. One example is the 'Sonoma' series from Irene Tolomeo in California; these peonies are especially noted for new color combinations and tones and combinations.

The Itoh hybrids are by and large sterile. When, eventually, a viable seed is produced, it may establish the next monumental step in producing a new fertile generation of exciting peonies.

'Bartzella' is as popular today as it was three decades ago when American nurseryman Roger Anderson introduced it.

Unnamed Garden Plants

Gardeners often have unnamed peonies, frequently as a beautiful pass-along from friends or a treasured living family heirloom dug from a parent's or grandparent's garden some many years ago. The desire to correctly name it is appreciated, but unless the flower is an exact match to a known named plant in a reputable book or at an established peony garden, confirming the correct name is almost impossible.

Many selections were commercially lost during World Wars I and II. During financial crises, as family nurseries failed, hundreds of acres were plowed under and turned to other crops. Meanwhile, ever-industrious bees have cross-pollinated countless garden peonies and no doubt in some cases these slightly different seedlings have grown up and replaced their parent plants.

While some peonies have distinctive characteristics, there are and were so many double pink peonies, for example, that identification of an unnamed one is problematic at best. There are no color photographs of the early peonies, many of the early descriptions are simply too vague ("our finest pink"), and there just aren't many other characteristics that are useful to sort the unknown peonies out. Fortunately, DNA fingerprinting may help resolve many of our garden unknowns in the future. So, if you have a peony you like and don't know its name, embrace it for the joy it provides you. If you must name it, give it a pet name that will keep a memory alive for generations to come.

Wild Species Not Common in Cultivation

Only two species, *Paeonia brownii* and *P. californica*, are native to North America. Both are found on the West Coast. Both are spring-bloomers and go dormant before the hot, searing summers arrive. This is an adaption to their native dry summer ecosystems. In cultivation, these species do best in mountainous areas with winter snow, superb drainage, and shelter from summer rains.

For gardeners living in such areas, these species are fine additions from the native flora for their botanical and ecological interest. Neither are ornamental as understood by most gardeners and consequently are little seen in most peony gardens. Both have flowers similar to hellebores, but only in the darker color values. These flowers are of no interest to commercial growers as the blooms are only about 2 inches (5 cm) across and have little color variation from the natural burgundy and gold.

Peony species from Asia and Europe can be appreciated in the garden where their simple flowers add pale pink to red tones. By contrast, *Paeonia mlokosewitschii* (or, Molly the witch, as it has long been known) is sometimes grown for its very early delicate yellow flowers and contrast of dull blue-gray rounded foliage. *Paeonia tenuifolia*, the fern-leaf peony, is beloved in rock gardens where its early flowers, small size, and delicate foliage help make pleasing garden compositions.

Some species from eastern Asia, like *Paeonia obovata*, are best handled as long-lived wildflowers for brightly lit openings in the woodland garden. By contrast, other species from sunnier habitats are more easily grown, such as *P. officinalis*, which our grandmothers generally called the Memorial Day peony, and *P. peregrina*, which imparts its brilliant cherry red tones to its offspring.

For the tree peonies, several species are of interest. One is *Paeonia rockii*, or Rock's peony, treasured for its petal's dark purple flares, or blotches. Indeed, in the many tree peony cultivars available, the dark flares are an indication that *P. rockii* is in the parentage.

Another tree peony species, recognized by Chinese experts as *Paeonia ostii*, is usually offered as the selection 'Phoenix White'. Leaving the taxonomy to be resolved by molecular fingerprinting, this long-appreciated peony is loved for its nearly pure white flowers. It is also a medicinal in some traditional Chinese medicines.

Paeonia lactiflora is the parent species of most bush peony cultivars, including 'Gay Paree'.

Kinds

of

Peonies

The categories and floral forms established by the American Peony Society have been used in the United States and Canada for decades and are used by most growers and gardeners worldwide. Category refers to the kind of peony, which determines its garden care. Floral form is about the kind of flowers, important for garden and floral design, but not so important for culture.

Plant Categories

Peony categories are based on parentage, not era of introduction or country of origin. There are five different groupings:

1   Species peonies are the undomesticated and beautiful plants found in nature.

2   Lactiflora peonies are derived from the Chinese herbaceous species *Paeonia lactiflora* or bred among its many cultivars.

3   Hybrids are herbaceous peonies involving one or more herbaceous peony parents outside of the Lactiflora group.

4   Itoh peonies are hybrids between tree peonies and herbaceous peonies. Technically, the Itoh hybrids are only the first four introduced: 'Yellow Crown', 'Yellow Dream', 'Yellow Emperor', and 'Yellow Heaven'. All the rest are intersectionals; however, common practice is to call all such hybrids Itoh peonies.

5   Tree peonies are selections derived from related woody species originally from China.

'Nosegay', single

'President Lincoln', single

Flower Forms

In order to discuss the great diversity of peony flowers, it is essential to organize them into floral groups, called forms. Peony floral forms established by the American Peony Society are based on the overall structure of the flower and how the floral parts relate to each other. The system works well for all herbaceous peonies. The top or terminal flower on a stem is the one that is evaluated since the side flowers can occasionally be slightly different.

The basic types are single, Japanese, anemone, bomb, semidouble, and double. The technical differences are based on the number of rows of petals, the condition of the guard petals (the outer row of petals), the presence of stamens and anthers (the parts that bear pollen), the partial to complete transformation of anthers to petals (at least as recognized by the typical gardener), and the reduction of the carpels (the potential seed-pods) to insignificance. The forms grade into each other, much like colors of the rainbow. However, the terms are essential to describe and understand the look of the flowers. These terms are everywhere in nursery catalogs and peony shows. An excellent, detailed, and illustrated series of articles on these forms is available online from the American Peony Society. The three-part series is called "Peony Flower Anatomy." A more complex set of floral forms is used in Asia, especially for tree peonies, and is sometimes encountered in specialty catalogs.

'Do Tell', Japanese

SINGLE PEONIES

Single peonies have one or two rows of large petals, a multitude of golden pollen-bearing anthers, and one to five carpels, where seed is formed. Single peonies look a bit like wild roses, only much bigger (and better). 'Krinkled White', 'Roselette', 'Scarlet Heaven' and 'Sea Shell' are all examples of single peonies.

JAPANESE AND ANEMONE PEONIES

Japanese and anemone peonies are similar to single peonies with one or two rows of petals, but their stamens and anthers have been transformed into narrow, petal-like structures. Japanese forms may show a trace of pollen but are usually not pollen-bearing. Anemone forms have anthers that become wider petal structures and no longer contain pollen. The two forms intergrade, but are separated as follows.

JAPANESE BLOOMS

The stamens of Japanese blooms are transformed into narrow, petal-like structures (staminodes). These staminodes retain shape, texture, and usually color features that belie their original origin as stamens. The flowers of some Japanese forms have a yellow center that looks like an egg yolk. 'Garden Lace', 'Mahogany', and 'Walter Mains' are among the well-known examples.

'Jean Ericksen', Japanese

'Gay Paree', anemone

ANEMONE BLOOMS

The stamens of anemone blooms are transformed into broader petal-like structures (petaloids.) These petaloids show no indication in shape or texture of being derived from stamens, although their color can be yellow to nearly matching the true petals. Some anemone forms have the overall effect of a sea urchin at the center of the flower. 'Belleville', 'Bouquet Perfect', and 'Gay Paree' are examples of anemone forms.

BOMB PEONIES

Bomb peonies are named for the mounded French ice-cream dessert served on a plate (bombe), and they are a feast for the eyes. Bomb forms represent the ultimate in the transformation of stamens to petal-like tissue, here called inner petals. The inner petals are convincingly petal-like, but form a beautifully dense petal-ball (the ice cream mound) that sits on the plate of guard (outer) petals. The guard petals can be the same or a different color than the inner petals.

'Touch of Class', anemone

'Red Charm', bomb

Among the many popular bomb-type peonies are 'Angel Cheeks', 'Big Ben', 'Bridal Shower', 'Monsieur Jules Elie', and 'Red Charm'.

SEMIDOUBLE PEONIES

Semidouble peonies have many rows of petals, with some stamens and anthers present among the many petals. What happened to the other stamens and anthers? They have been transformed into the extra petals. The carpels may be normal or reduced in size and number. Among the best known semidoubles are 'Buckeye Belle', 'Coral Sunset', and 'Garden Treasure'.

DOUBLE PEONIES

In double peonies, all the stamens and anthers are transformed into large petals that are nearly identical in size. In some cases, the carpels are completely transformed, too. Beginners sometimes confuse double peonies with bombs: bombs are easily recognized by the plate of guard petals, whereas in all the doubles the petals are delightfully similar. This is a very large group of peonies, and even a short roll-call begins with 'Bowl of Cream', 'Chestine Gowdy', 'Duchesse de Nemours', 'Kansas', and 'Mrs. Franklin D. Roosevelt' followed by many, many more.

'Pink Pearl', double

ABOVE LEFT 'Mrs. Franklin
D. Roosevelt', double

Joining a peony club or society will put you in contact with other peony enthusiasts, many of whom love to share their knowledge. You'll also hear about new introductions; get advice on peony culture, care, and best practices; and meet a world of friends. Most likely you'll end up swapping choice plants, too. And be certain to travel to peony shows; there is much to learn from colleagues and it's an inspiration to see so many flowers at their best. It's glamour we can all aspire to and reach.

'Cora Louise', semidouble

The Joy

of

Gardening

Gloriously blooming peonies have no equal in the garden. Their colors, forms, fragrances, and range of plant sizes present the gardener an unrivaled palette for creative expression. It's hard to think of another kind of plant that offers such variety, from the boldly colored flowers and lacy foliage of fern-leaf peonies through the numerous floral hues, foliage textures, and growth habits of bush, intersectional, and tree peonies. For the sense—and scents—of romance, peonies take first place in our hearts and minds. Anyone who has ever walked into a garden of fragrant peonies or quaffed the aroma of peonies in bouquets has a memory for life.

Every garden has room for peonies. If there's only room for one, opt for a diva like 'Angel Cheeks' that stars across many roles. If there's room for more than a few, consider how peonies will be featured in your garden and shared with family and friends.

Gardeners who adore their peonies tend toward two camps. One group plants all their peonies together, whether that takes one bed, many beds, or even the entire garden. The other group integrates peonies with other ornamental plants throughout the garden. Either approach is beautiful, and either leads up to the next issue for gardeners to consider: aim for a concentrated peony bloom period or an extended one?

A monochromatic design creates strong visual impact, as seen in this pink trio that includes 'Leslie Peck', a paler colored peony, and lupines.

Deep blue delphiniums (foreground) and iris (background) balance the vivid pink flowers of 'Edulis Superba' in this harmonious vignette.

Place Peonies as Highlights

A key element in peony enjoyment is surprisingly simple: determine where you and your guests will be when you enjoy your peonies and plant them there. How we experience peonies is quite different depending on our distance from them, our speed or pace, and our ability to slow down, stop, and even linger.

When driving by a garden with peonies, we see colorful flashes and swirling flowers, but their detail and wafting fragrance are essentially missed. If we need a drive-by showstopper, by all means go for a flower with bold colors.

By contrast, up close and intimate in the garden is quite a different experience. It's nuanced and totally personal, the kind of encounter and memory that comes from walking among beds filled entirely with peonies, or peonies intermingled with iris, columbines, and flowering bulbs.

Somewhere between is the view from the dining room window or a bedroom that an elderly relative calls home. Yet, even this can be a featured view, complemented with daily bouquets that bring the best of the panorama, the glowing presence of the peony flowers, indoors.

'Coral Sunset' shines in front of a dark-leaved shrub accompanied by pink, yellow, and purple lupines.

White, red, and pink peonies mingle in this cheerful border.

A garden requires more than highlights; it also has to have harmonizing elements. Many heirloom bush peonies feature pastel floral tones rather than dazzling contemporary color notes. These heirloom cultivars are unrivaled for setting a romantic mood, especially when the flowers are fragrant. They are equally indispensable for complementing other floral colors, so include the classic peonies and the modern cultivars with coordinating tones to strengthen the "punch" of the showstopping peonies you treasure.

When deciding how best to place peonies to suit your needs, especially if you have many garden views to consider, take a cue from the dramatic arts. Two approaches are possible. Do you want an explosion of peonies, an annual event of stunning magnificence? Or do you prefer a peony theater that can extend over a three- to five-week season? An event approach to peony gardening makes for an unforgettable experience, in part because it is as intensely spectacular as it is ephemeral. It works well if there is a special date to anchor the season. By contrast, the theatrical approach allows you to savor the garden and return over several days, refreshed with a related but different scene of the seasonal production.

Success with the theater approach requires thoughtfully sequencing the bloom performance. For herbaceous peonies, the season can be heralded with a bold intersectional or 'Red Charm', broadened by the chromatic chorus (add more herbaceous hybrids here including corals), expanded with a cast of classic fragrant peonies, and culminated with the appearance of stunning floral divas. The theater closes with a finale of the last peonies of the season, usually very late doubles. Each region will have its own best selection, but the framework is the same. Think dramatically and your selections will be fine.

Coral, red, pink, and white peonies in a mixed border.

A pastel-colored peony plays a supporting role when paired with a strong, deep rich red peony.

When paired with white and pale-colored peonies, the pastel-colored peony now becomes a focal point in the border.

Once the approach is decided, then the choice of whether or not to add other perennials becomes clearer. The prime advantage of planting beds of only peonies, regardless of the choice of an event- or a season-based approach, is that the garden is simply sensational in bloom. You and your guests will be speechless. The floral fragrances are intensified by the contribution of related but distinct floral notes, each accenting the others.

If there is a special date around the time of year when your bed of peonies is in bloom, it's clear where people will gather and linger. After all, if you have a peony garden like this, it's so much fun to flaunt it. Cutting several blooms for the home or table, or to take to a convalescent relative unable to come to the garden, if done judiciously, leaves the floral extravaganza intact.

After the peony bloom period, the peony bed is supremely low maintenance for the rest of the garden season. Your garden energies can be placed elsewhere, like the vegetable garden. Perhaps you can even go on vacation.

The virtues of a mixed-border design, whether event- or season-based, are also many. You can arrange a series of drop-dead floral vignettes in the garden, such as pink peonies and blue iris, white peonies with creamy yellow foxgloves, or red peonies ballooning over silvery foliage of lambs-ears. Use our suggested list of companion plants to let your imagination soar. Since some garden seasons are always ahead of or behind others, if there is an important date to celebrate, the mixed-border design can allow for more robust confidence that at least one part of the garden will be exquisite on your special date.

'Coral Charm' bridges the height gap between lupines and a crabapple tree.

'Lovely Rose' peony and purple irises draw attention to a whimsical garden statue.

Plant for the Garden's Lifetime

When considering where to plant peonies, it is important to think long-term. Of all garden perennials and shrubs, peonies have among the highest potential to be very long-lived. In established peony gardens, it's not uncommon to have many peonies growing exactly where they were planted decades earlier. There are well-documented cases of herbaceous peonies living for over a century with minimal care. And who hasn't driven past an old field where the bush peonies are the last signs that this was once a place called home? As to the endurance of tree peonies, reliable reports from China confirm they can live for centuries and become venerable specimens.

BEWARE OF SHADE-CREEP

Shade-creep is a slow and sly design concern. Peonies do best in full sun and can thrive in the same site for more than one hundred years. The shade zone cast by a tree in the year it is planted is very different from the shade zone ten, twenty, or even thirty years ahead. Ideally, gardeners should plant peonies where there won't be shade for at least a human generation. However, not everyone plans gardens this way and that becomes especially evident when homes change owners.

Too often, the new owner of an established home finds peonies that don't flower, and the culprit is almost always too much shade. Usually a previous owner planted the peonies in full sun, but since then, trees have grown to shade the site. As a result, the peonies bloom poorly, if at all. Fertilizing doesn't help. Only moving the peonies to a site in full sun corrects the problem.

Similar unanticipated changes that cast shade and lead to poor performance of peonies may include adding a new room to a house or putting a second floor, as over the garage. This is especially problematic when the changed structure belongs to a neighbor. It's time to move these peonies. Whether you are redesigning a new garden or new to your current home, look to the long-term shade issues as you design and consider some of the site-appropriate compatible plants suggested later in this chapter.

TREE PEONIES ARE THE CROWN JEWELS OF SPRING

Tree peonies complement and can be planted with herbaceous and intersectional peonies, although they are often planted separately since their bloom season can begin earlier than the other kinds of peonies. This spatial separation reflects how some aspects of Japanese, Chinese, and Korean garden aesthetics and traditions became woven into Western garden styles.

'Shima-nishiki', a striped tree peony, and a variegated hosta decorate a neutral stucco house wall.

Some garden references of the twentieth century used plantings of tree peonies to introduce Asian themes and decorated these plantings with lanterns, pools, and stepping-stone paths. This is certainly a respectful approach, but tree peonies need not be limited to this one role. Indeed, tree peonies are robust enough to fit almost every garden style.

As with herbaceous peonies, tree peonies thrive in full sun. Their flowers, while relatively fleeting, persist best with some afternoon shade, making tree peonies ideal for garden locations where they are slightly protected.

Tree peonies are especially useful in transition areas between perennial garden beds and more shaded areas. They excel in compositions with partial-shade plantings of shrubs such as azaleas and rhododendrons (*Rhododendron*), pearlbush (*Exochorda racemosa*), and small trees like corylopsis (*Corylopsis*), silverbell tree (*Halesia*), many kinds of dogwoods (*Cornus*), and redbud (*Cercis*). In all cases, reliable blooming requires sun at least two-thirds of the day, preferably more, with morning sun exposure being ideal.

'Bartzella' peony in a mixed border backed by purple maples and dark green conifers.

Peony borders line both sides of a serpentine turf path.

Strawberry-red blooms with ruffled petals and dark center flares adorn 'Banquet', a tree peony with attractive cut-leaf foliage.

Season Progressions

Pairing peonies with other plants, in and out of bloom, makes sensational floral and foliage combinations throughout the season. Do not overlook the early spring season, for as peony shoots emerge from the soil and begin to grow, their colors are remarkable. Take inspiration from Monet's garden at Giverney, where the artist intentionally placed complementary-colored pansies and tulips to play with the young peony stem colors, which are cultivars that usually begin emerging a deep maroon. It's an absolutely remarkable sight and takes the peonies and tulips to new heights. Since the tulips and pansies are annuals and are removed once they finish blooming, they do not compete with the peonies for sun and space during the summer growing period.

It's tempting just to use seasonally fleeting perennials such as Virginia bluebells (*Mertensia virginiana*) and some nonaggressive small bulbs like crocus (*Crocus*) and Roman hyacinths (*Hyacinthus orientalis*), but depending on your region, the foliage may start dying and yellowing when the peonies are in full bloom.

Since there are few notes anywhere comparing emergent peony stem colors, look in your own garden and take advantage of the peonies you have. Your peony stems may emerge in tones of light green to deep maroon. Then plan for next year with pansies, tulips, and other spring annuals to extend the garden season among the peonies you already treasure. To add more color variety, visit peony gardens about two months before bloom to see peony stem colors and decide which peonies could be added in your garden for the effect you desire.

Red peony stems and young foliage emerging through Siberian bugloss (*Brunnera macrophylla*) and annual honesty (*Lunaria annua*).

After blooming, peonies play a special role. It may seem heretical, but peonies excel in being green backgrounds, launching eruptions of late-season lilies like *Lilium regale* and cultivars such as 'Casa Blanca', balloon flowers (*Platycodon grandiflora*), the sword-shaped foliage of Byzantine gladiolus (*Acidanthera* 'Muriale'), florist's gladiolas (*Gladiolus* cultivars), montbretias (as *Crocosmia* 'Lucifer'), and roses. Summer annuals with hot colors and nonintensive water needs such as flowering tobaccos (*Nicotiana*), some salvias (*Salvia*), and zinnias (*Zinnia*) delightfully and perfectly fill gaps among the peony foliage.

As the first hints of fall colors creep into the leaves of trees and shrubs, it's the season for blue-flowered monkshoods (*Aconitum carmichelii*) to be combined with Japanese anemones, such as 'Honorine Jobert', for bubbles of blue and white that shimmer above the bush peony foliage when most of the garden world is focusing on fall clean-up. If there is part shade nearby, toad lilies (*Tricrytis*) add jeweled shapes and tones. All three sail boldly and in full bloom right into the first frigid blasts of approaching winter. It's deeply pleasing to have the farewell to the growing season hoisted high over peony foliage and with it the promise of friendships celebrated over winter feasts to come.

Peonies Make It Special

Peonies are ideal to establish the garden's mood for a celebratory day, such as a wedding or an anniversary. For the special day, ideally you'll start planning at least three years out, since peonies can take that much time to establish full blooming strength. If the wedding or event is planned on shorter notice, recognize that the plants won't have had time to establish to bloom abundantly, so you'll need to supplement your flowers and bouquets with additional peonies from friends and florists.

As years pass and your peonies mature, having your festive garden of peonies allows you to start a new tradition with family and friends. One way is to routinely host a Peonies-Are-Blooming party. If someone in the extended network of family and friends is planning a special day, propose hosting a prewedding party, or even the wedding ceremony itself, in your garden. Consider hosting a photo-shoot in your garden as your meaningful gift of memories. Having a peony garden in which to host parties is great fun. Everyone, including the community of passers-by, benefits.

There is another reason peonies are so loved. For generations across North America, wherever bush peonies were grown, they became "the" flower for decorating graves on Memorial Day, or as it was once known, Decoration Day. Even now, some guests who visit our gardens or see particular peonies in bouquets can recall the civic ceremonies, school programs, or family activities that respected the sacrifices and memories of those no longer with us, helping the reminiscences flow.

With the transition to all-lawn memorial gardens after the mid-twentieth century, the practice of planting meaningful perennials, especially bush peonies, has declined, yet this is one tradition not only to be cherished, but renewed. Let's start now, even with peony plantings at home. Carol has long shown the way, by taking cut peonies to care homes where we can honor heroes and heroines still among us as well as awaken memories ages old.

Grasses form a backdrop for yellow peonies

A–Z of Companion Plants

While our lists of companion plants are mostly of perennials, roses have to be heralded. Roses and peonies are simply exquisite companions, whether in the garden or in bouquets. As backdrops to peony beds as in the Peony Garden at Nichols Arboretum in Michigan, shrub roses and climbing roses on posts, arbors, or enclosing fences have no rivals. Modern groundcover roses add a great deal of potential for gardeners willing to experiment with them among their peonies. Reblooming roses may have their first bloom period overlap with some of the later-flowering bush peonies.

Many reliable perennials work well with peonies. If you grow any of the plants in the following lists, consider adding peonies, too. This list is based on our decades of experience and extensive travel to see peony gardens. Since peonies grow well and begin blooming from early spring in zone 8 and by early summer right into zone 3, each garden and climate will tend to a different set of these perennials. Match peony bloom times with these perennials based on your experience and what you see locally. When in doubt, try the combination yourself.

One of the great pleasures of combination planting is the rich variation in foliage. There are so many shades of green, leaf textures, shapes, and leaf postures on the plant, they provide a widely varied palette with flowers as the great bonus.

Purple iris complement red peonies.

PERENNIALS THAT TYPICALLY BLOOM OR COMBINE WELL WITH PEONIES

These perennials are first considerations for their ability to mix with bush, intersectional, or tree peonies. The concurrent bloom periods will vary from year to year across zones 3–8.

Alchemilla, lady's mantle

Aquilegia, columbine. Stunning in bloom with peonies.

Astrantia major, masterwort

Baptisia, false indigo, wild indigo

Brunnera, Siberian bugloss

Campanula, bellwort, campanula

Centaurea cyaneus, cornflower, bachelor button

Convallaria majalis, lily of the valley. For naturalizing near tree peonies where there is part shade.

Delphinium, larkspur

Dianthus, pinks, sweet William

Dicentra, bleeding hearts. So romantic in bloom!

Digitalis, foxglove. These were made for peony borders and bouquets.

Fragaria, strawberry. Break the rules: use strawberry as a groundcover near tree peonies.

Geranium, geranium, cranesbill. These are the hardy perennials, not the florist's or zonal geraniums.

Gypsophila repens, baby's breath. Little else provides such fine clouds of white flowers.

Iris, iris. Peonies and iris are the classic and eternal twins of the perennial border.

Leucanthemum, Shasta daisy. The crisply clean flowers are a perfect complement to peonies.

Lupinus, lupine. Stunning spikes of blue, white, pink, yellow, and even bicolored flowers accent peonies like few other flowers.

Papaver, poppy

Salvia, salvia

Tiarella, foam flower, false miterwort

Viola, pansy, violet

PERENNIALS THAT BLOOM AT OTHER SEASONS AND LOOK GREAT WITH PEONY FOLIAGE

These perennials are beautiful in bloom. Use peony foliage to heighten their attraction. Their foliage is also attractive when peonies bloom.

Aconitum carmichelii, aconite, monkshood

Amsonia, bluestar

Anemone ×hupehensis, Japanese anemone

Aruncus, goat's beard. The foliage adds a wildness that is needed when large peony plantings are intended to be informal.

Asarum, wild ginger

Aster, aster. 'Purple Dome' is well proportioned.

Astilbe pumila, astilbe

Bergenia cordifolia, bergenia

Calamentha, calamentha. Combines well with peonies and roses.

Clematis heracleifolia and *C. recta*, bush clematis

Epimedium, barrenwort

Helleborus, hellebore, Christmas rose. An ideal, long-lived evergreen perennial companion to tree peonies.

Hemerocallis, daylily. Modern cultivars can be used among the bush peonies if, and only if, the selections form slow-growing clumps.

Heuchera, alumroot, coral bells

Iberis sempervirens, candy tuft

Nepeta, catmint

Phlox, phlox

Playtcodon, balloon flowers

Sedum, sedum

Stachys byzantina, lamb's ears

Thermopsis caroliniana, false lupine

Tricyrtis, toad lily

Veronica, speedwell. Most useful are any of the many low to ground-covering ones.

Veronicastrum, Culver's root

Waldsteinia, barrrenwort

PEONIES AND BULBS

Bush peonies and ornamental onions (*Allium* species and cultivars) create sensational combinations. You'll have to experiment with the cultivars of both the peonies and onions to get the synchronized bloom for your area. Hedge your bets and plant an overlapping bloom time of both and most years you'll have at least one showstopping combination.

Early spring bulbs that bloom long before peony season, such as crocus (*Crocus*), dwarf iris (*Iris danfordae*), and snowdrops (*Galanthus nivalis*), can be planted near peonies, but they should not be allowed to overrun the peonies. Weed out excess bulbs. Aggressive spring bulbs, such as the white-flowered star of Bethlehem (*Ornathogalum*) or the blue squills (*Scilla*), may be too successful and become pests.

Delicate, pastel-colored 'Sea Shell' peony and starry *Allium cristophii* are a spectacular duo in the garden.

Allium, ornamental onion. Experiment boldly!

Alstroemeria, Peruvian lily

Colchicum, fall crocus

Crocosmia, montbretia. 'Lucifer' is the best known and most widely grown.

Eremurus, foxtail lily

Fritillaria persica, Persian fritillary

Leucoma ostium, giant or summer snowflake

Lilium, lily. Ornamental lilies are splendid arising among peony plants.

Narcissus, jonquils, narcissus

Sternberg lutea, winter daffodil

Several tender bulbs work well as annuals among bush peonies, provided they are far enough from the peonies that the roots aren't disturbed. For fragrance, Abyssinian gladiolus (*Acidanthera* 'Muriale') is a delight with its airy white flowers carried aloft on thin stems. More familiar are florists glads (*Gladiolus*) in their complete riot of colors. One way to include these glads is to start them in groups in large plastic pots that hold at least a gallon of planting mix and add more holes to the bottom. Start them in a bright area along a driveway or side of the building. Just as the roots begin to grow out of the bottom, move the pots, without removing the glads, to shallow holes in gaps among the bush peonies. The glads will need staking, but the effect is spectacular!

The two-tone peony and dark background beckon a companion planting.

SOME ANNUALS TO CONSIDER

These annuals will add eye-popping color to any vacant spaces in peony beds without requiring extensive watering, which the peonies dislike. All of them are easy to remove at the end of the season without disturbing the peonies.

Calendula, pot marigold

Capsicum cultivars, dwarf ornamental peppers

Escholtzia californica, California poppy

Nicotiana, fragrant tobacco

Portulaca grandiflora, rose moss

Salvia coccinea, Texas salvia

Salvia ×superba, garden salvias

Tagetes, marigold

Verbena bonariensis, purple vervain

Zinnia, zinnia

SOME PLANTS TO AVOID

Peonies of all kinds perform best without unmanaged groundcovers that run deep into their root systems. These problem plants include leadwort (*Ceratostigma plumbaginoides*), ivy (*Hedera*), and pachysandra (*Pachysandra terminalis*). Avoid the truly aggressive campanulas like *Campanula punctata*, or *C. rapunculoides*, as their creeping rhizomes will run through the bush peonies and be difficult to control. Likewise, so-called low maintenance perennials, such as bishop's weed (*Aegopodium*), crown vetch (*Coronaria varia*), or old-fashioned orange daylilies (*Hemerocallis fulva*), form smothering masses that overwhelm the peonies in time. It's guaranteed you'll resort to digging up the area to tease out the rootlets.

Planting

and

Care

Success with peonies is simple. First, be in a climate with cold winter temperatures. Then, give peonies a well-drained site with at least six hours of sun. Finally, grow them where they have good air circulation and without competition from grass, shrubs, or trees. It's that easy.

If you do this, how well may they grow? At the historic Peony Garden of the Nichols Arboretum, which celebrates its centennial in 2022, many of the herbaceous peonies are thriving right where they were originally planted nearly a century ago.

Peony Success—Just the Facts

1. Be in a winter-cold climate.
2. Obtain good-quality roots or plants.
3. Select a well-drained site.
4. Provide at least six hours of direct sun.
5. Insure good air circulation.
6. Remove competing plants.

Once you've selected a site for your peonies, follow these planting basics and your plants will thrive: purchase or acquire good quality roots or plants; plant them in rich, well-drained soils that never have standing water; allow each a 3-foot (91-cm) space; plant herbaceous peonies shallowly, with the buds only 1–2 inches (2.5–5 cm) beneath the soil surface; and plant grafted tree peonies with the graft buried deeply. The rest of this chapter provides details for success.

Selecting the Site

CLIMATE

Peonies need cold winter climates to grow well. Generally, this can be found across USDA hardiness zones 3 to 8, where average winter temperatures range from -40°F to 20°F (-40°C to -7°C). As a rule, if lilacs (*Syringa*), apples, or flowering crabapples (both are *Malus*) thrive in the region, then any peony should be fine.

SOIL FERTILITY AND DRAINAGE

All peonies need fertile, well-drained soils with a pH close to 6.5. Fertility is mineral richness, not just organic content. Drainage is essential, since wet roots in the winter are likely to rot. A peony root is similar to a carrot, which will rot if left in water for an extended period. Nature's trick is that wild peonies are usually found on mineral-rich soils on hillsides or on well-drained soils that are clay-rich or stony scree, while woodland peonies are in duff-rich soils. All these situations are quite different from cold, moist pondside or riverside soils.

'Gardenia' flowers have a blush coloration when weather is cloudy, but sunny conditions cause a white bloom. The unopened bud may have a few red streaks that are not visible once the bloom opens.

Most peonies require six hours of direct sunlight per day.

In the garden, sandy soils will benefit from the addition of organic matter to help retain moisture and add nutrition. Clay soils have mineral richness but may need amending to help with drainage. Any organic matter that will gradually decompose and leave air spaces is helpful.

One method to overcome the difficulty of drainage of heavy soils is to loosen the soil to the depth of a shovel blade. This reduces the compactness of the heavy clay. Make sure the loosened soil is level with the adjoining untouched soil. Place the bare root in the center and pull soil up from all sides to make a moat around the root. The moat, which is below the level of the root, will catch and hold excess water.

LIGHT

As a rule, peonies do best in full sunlight, which means six hours or more of sunlight per day. For bush peonies, the abundance, quality, and strength of stem are reduced as the shade increases. Morning sun and afternoon shade work well to keep the hottest sun from the blooms, helping them last a bit longer than if in total full day sun. The same is true for tree peonies. That is why you often see parasols positioned over oriental peonies in photos, providing that extra bit of afternoon shade to prolong the flowering.

Light in any garden usually changes over the years. A site with full sun fifteen years ago may now be in part shade from trees that are growing to maturity. Likewise, removing or trimming trees may bring more sun into the garden.

It is tempting to plant peonies in new beds where they are close to young trees and revel in the garden's success for several years. Do so with the understanding that within a few years some of the peonies will need to be transplanted into full sun.

Planting

SOIL PREPARATION

Loosen the soil to a sufficient depth and width to accommodate a mature peony; an area 2 feet deep and 3 feet wide (60 by 91 cm) is sufficient. If the soil is heavy clay, mix in some potting soil or compost. Next, mix a handful of bulb fertilizer into the bottom of the hole, covering it with some soil to prevent the roots from coming in direct contact with the fertilizer. A combination of bone meal and potash may be used in place of a commercial fertilizer. A low-nitrogen fertilizer is best. The fertilizer used should have a smaller first number (nitrogen) than the following numbers. Do not use quick-release fertilizers; what is needed is the slow-release of nutrients from the compost and/or fertilizers as the plant establishes.

ROOT PLACEMENT

Put peony roots in the ground as soon as possible after receiving them in the fall. The roots will keep for several days in the packing materials if you need to prepare a planting spot. If the roots appear dry, soak them in water for a few hours to rehydrate them.

Peonies emerge with red stems that turn green as the leaves begin to open.

Once the hole is dug, place the root's eyes pointing upward at the center of the planting site. The eye color will be white, pink, or red, and the eye will be about the size of the tip of a little finger. The eyes will become the center of the plant and new roots will fill out the circle around them. The peony eyes, being the growing points, will become the stems with leaves and flowers in the spring.

Lay the root piece flat on the soil, or if it has multiple legs, stand them so the eyes are pointed up, and cover it with soil. Eyes will reorient themselves to point to the sun, so if some eyes are pointing down or sideways, don't be concerned.

Cover root and eyes with soil. There should be only 2 inches (5 cm) of soil over the eyes even in cold climates, 1 inch (2.5 cm) in warmer-winter climates. Deep planting may reduce the bloom.

Water the area to settle the soil. Water more if needed due to current moisture conditions. Note that none of the plant will be visible above ground until it begins to grow next year in early spring, so you may want to mark the spot where it is planted. Any accompanying nametag can be removed from the root and secured in the soil nearby.

Expect only one or two stems, each 6–8 inches (15–20 cm) tall, the first spring as most of the root's stored energy is being sent to form the feeder roots that will take up the moisture and nutrients necessary to sustain the plant for its lifetime. The number of stems should double the next year and the plant should be quite full and bloom well by the third season.

Ongoing Care

WATER

In the first year after planting, a peony may need supplemental watering as it continues to form the fine roots that are essential to the plant's endurance. This is especially true in areas where there is little summer rain.

Once established in areas where summer rain is the norm, peonies may not need supplemental water. It is a surprise to many visitors that the Peony Garden at the University of Michigan's Nichols Arboretum has never had a manual or automatic irrigation system since it was established in 1922.

Overwatering from automatic lawn sprinkling systems can be a problem for all types of peonies. Such overwatering can exacerbate peony fungal diseases and, in some cases, lead to fatal root rot over the following winter. Allow the soil to dry somewhat between irrigation episodes.

ANNUAL FERTILIZING

Fertilize peonies as the new shoots emerge from the soil in early spring. If that time is missed, then fertilize in late fall when you cut down the foliage. Time the application before a rainfall, which will help incorporate the fertilizer into the soil.

Use a fertilizer with the balance of nitrogen below that of the other elements. Bulb fertilizers for tulips and daffodils are good examples of acceptable peony fertilizers. Avoid lawn fertilizers, as these are manufactured to have a high nitrogen content that promotes lush growth which is attractive to the fungus botrytis. Organic gardeners who annually add compost to the soil should watch that the soil does not build up too high around the crown. One way is to keep the compost towards the drip line. Once eyes on the peony root are more than 3–6 inches (8–15 cm) below soil level, the plants may not bloom well.

Organic gardeners can apply a dilute fish-emulsion to the foliage *after* the peonies have bloomed, but before midsummer. Later applications may interfere with winter dormancy and are to be avoided. Since fish emulsions will make the garden pungent for several days, schedule the application almost a week before you host any social event in the garden.

SPRING CLEANUP AND WEEDING

Check all the peony plantings and beds to remove any debris that may have accumulated over the plants. As the shoots emerge, check for signs of botrytis (see Diseases section following).

Weed control will be needed at times. Trifluralin, the chief ingredient in Preen, may be used for weed and grass control in peony beds, but avoid using the herbicide dichlobenil (trade name Casoron), as it also kills peonies. Check with your local garden center for instructions on chemical use.

For organic gardeners, the best weed control method is hand-pulling. Another is hoeing, chopping off very young weeds with their roots. A disadvantage of hoeing is that the peony roots may be damaged in the process.

Another organic weed control method is to spread an organic mulch between the peonies and allow it to slowly decompose into the beds. Place the mulch towards the drip-line rather than piled on the stems to prevent botrytis in moist years.

STAKING FLOWERS

Staking depends on the cultivar. Some peonies won't ever need staking, whereas many of the historic or large-flowered lactiflora peonies will always need it. If you don't ever want to stake your peonies, then select only peonies that don't require staking such as those with an Award of Landscape Merit designation by the American Peony Society. This will simplify your life, but you'll miss some of the classic fragrant bush peonies.

When needed, staking can be done in several ways, all of which are effective. One way is to place commercially available peony supports or peony rings over the plants before they reach the ring height. The stems will grow right through the supporting grids. This system has the advantage of being hidden when the peonies are in bloom. One risk is that it's tempting to put the supports too low to the ground since it looks better during the time it takes for the peonies to grow through and cover the supports.

Another way of staking is to surround plants with slender stakes of bamboo, cane, or even strong twigs. You can use several stakes around the perimeter of the entire bush, making a twine loop (or loops) to support the entire plant.

When spectacular flowers are needed, you might stake individual stems rather than an entire plant. In either case, the stakes do not need to rise to the full height of the flowers, and if the stakes are dyed green, they will be hardly noticeable. In some cases, just tying twine around the entire bush can work, with the plant supporting itself.

DISBUDDING

There's no pleasure quite like that of making stunning bouquets using flowers from your own garden. For showstopping peonies, this means each stem should have only one flower bud, the top one. Disbudding is the removal of all the side buds from every flower stem before they are the size of peas. Removing the side buds allows the plant to put all its energy into the terminal or largest bud on each flowering stem. The resulting flowers are spectacular.

Most of the historic (pre-1950) bush peonies from *P. lactiflora* have a number of side buds on each stem. The center bud will bloom first, then the side buds will bloom, often as a little bouquet (remove the central flower once it is past). Unfortunately, the large, full double blooms with their sidebuds can become so heavy, especially after a rainy spell, that they lay on the ground and are quite unsightly. Supports can be used but removing side buds will lessen the weight on the stem to help keep the stem upright. In addition, the terminal flower will grow larger since it doesn't have to share the nutrient and water supply with the smaller buds. Blooms for special occasions or for show flowers should have the side buds removed.

Many of the new hybrid varieties don't need to be disbudded since they don't have the weight issue: often they have only one bloom per stem or just a couple of side buds. Likewise, peonies with a single row of petals need not be disbudded.

The intersectional and tree peonies do not need to be disbudded, as their stem strength is sufficient and glorious side blooms seem not diminished in size or quality.

DEADHEADING

Deadheading is cutting off peony flowers that are past their prime so that the plant doesn't waste energy producing seeds and pods (assuming they are fertile). Deadheading will also tidy up the garden. Remove the spent flower just above the first three-lobed leaf or at a height that will attractively shape the plant.

For tree peonies, this is a time to consider cutting out any weak or scraggly branches so that the plant puts its energy into new growth where you want it. Trimming or shaping tree peonies just after bloom will preserve flower buds for the following season, whereas trimming in fall may remove flower buds.

FALL CLEANUP

Fall cleanup helps you have healthy plants the following spring. Rake up and dispose of fallen tree peony leaves. The woody stems of the tree peony remain to leaf out again in spring. However, bush peonies and intersectional peonies should have the foliage cut off clear to the ground. Leaving stubs above ground can allow the hollow stems to fill with sitting water which can rot the crown of the plant.

Although you might find buds above ground on intersectionals, we cut them down as there are plenty of underground buds available to grow next year. Place the removed foliage in the garbage. Rake up all of the fallen leaves and dispose of them offsite, too. This will reduce the number of botrytis spores available to attack your peonies in a wet spring. Home composting is *not recommended* since composting is likely not hot enough to kill the botrytis spores.

Container Growing

Peonies are *not* recommended for container growing because of the shape and structure of their root systems, as well as the damaging toll of winter freezing. Unlike roots in the ground which only freeze as the cold penetrates from above, in a container, the cold (and thaw) comes from all sides. This wreaks havoc on the roots as they transition to and from dormancy.

If you do attempt to grow peonies in containers, use a large planter, such as a half-barrel. Such containers will be difficult to move and take up a great deal of space in return for a short blooming period.

As to the tree peonies in ornamental pots that are seen in Chinese art, these were likely planted in anticipation of their stunning bloom and discarded once exhausted or then planted into the ground. There are also small-statured tree peonies with full-size flowers that could fit this role but are little seen outside of China as they are not prolific bloomers.

Pests and Diseases

Even though peonies are relatively disease-free, there are times when plants will be afflicted by problems. The most common problem with peonies is the soil-borne fungus botrytis.

Botrytis is sometimes called gray mold and comes in several strains, some specific to peonies. Symptoms include sudden wilting of leaves, stems that rot off at ground level, and small, hard, and blackened flower buds where there should be glorious flowers, the very essence of depravity in plant diseases. Stems may also show infections as dead zones. Later in the season there will be small "brown measles" on the leaves, even though other parts of the leaf surface are fine. All these are manifestations of botrytis.

Botrytis in both standing and falling stems.

BELOW LEFT Leaf botrytis.

Blackened flower buds are a sure sign of botrytis.

Diseased foliage with "measles"

Fortunately, botrytis is relatively easy to manage in the home garden. Garden sprays that control black spot in roses can be applied at 7- to 10-day intervals from first detection until bloom. For chemical controls, contact your local garden center or extension service.

For all gardeners (not just organic gardeners), since botrytis is not active year-round in the peonies, an important part of control is to break the botrytis life cycle. Do this by removing the diseased parts before the disease spreads further. For the blackened flower buds, as they are noted, cut the stems several inches below the last diseased part of the stem. Burn these diseased stems or put them in the trash and sanitize your tools before further use. Do not compost diseased portions in your yard or you risk reinfecting peonies at a later season. Early in the fall, as the peony leaves begin to go dormant, cut all the stems off at ground level and dispose offsite or burn. This essential part of fall cleanup removes any diseased plant material as a source of infection next spring.

Tree peonies can be afflicted by peony wilt of unknown source. Remove the affected branch and then sanitize your tools.

Root knot nematodes are occasional but serious problems of peonies. Symptoms are stunting of the plants and pea-sized nodules on the roots. For the home gardener, the best approach (after confirming the problem with one of the peony web sites at the end of this book) is to dig up the plants and their surrounding soil, dispose of them (not in the compost), replace the soil, and try another kind of plant (not peonies), or even turf the area for several years.

There are less frequently encountered peony diseases, and the web resources of both the American and Canadian Peony Societies are excellent places to begin for diagnosis, pictures, and recommendations of what to do.

ANTS

Ants are not a problem from the peony's perspective. They are naturally attracted to the small amounts of sugary sap secreted near and at the edges of peony buds. Removing ants from peonies to be used in bouquets is simple. Once the stem is cut, turn it upside down and gently flick the stem with a fingersnap to dislodge the ants, or quickly immerse the flower head in water to remove the ants. Granular hydramethylnon (trade name Amdro) can be sprinkled beneath the plant if there is an overabundance of ants.

Purchasing and Propagating

All types of peonies are usually purchased from mail-order sources for fall delivery as dormant roots. Some nurseries and garden centers sell potted peonies through the growing season. These potted plants should be placed in your garden soon after they arrive. Reputable nurseries send bush peony roots that are well developed and with at least three eyes. Beware of truly low-cost peonies as these are likely to have small roots and will bloom poorly, if at all, for years, since they will need to devote all their energy to making more roots instead of pleasing you with blooms.

Honey bee about to land on 'The Mackinac Grand'

Bush peonies are easily divided in the fall by taking divisions of the mother plant. For success, these divisions should be the length and size of a large carrot and should have three eyes. The eyes are the visible but dormant buds. The larger eyes will give rise to next year's stems, leaves, and flowers, while the smaller eyes may wait for future seasons.

If the root mass is too small, the food supply can be diminished the first year before the plant has been able to make the fine roots that take up water and nutrients. If the root mass is too large, the plant will sit and sulk and not do much because it has not been given the appropriate signal that it needs to grow. Although root pieces with fewer eyes will grow, they will take more years to make a sizable plant. The stem count usually doubles or triples each year until the plant reaches a 3-foot (91-cm) width.

For tree peonies sold via catalog, it is important to distinguish between own-root versus grafted plants. If the nursery or garden center cannot tell you which it is, assume the plant is grafted. Own-root plants are preferred and worth the extra price. As their name implies, own-root tree peony cultivars are rooted pieces of one cultivar. This way if anything happens to the growing top, the stems sent up from the root will be the same cultivar you purchased.

By contrast, grafted tree peonies are made from two kinds of peonies. The aboveground part is the cultivar the gardener wants. The roots, however, are usually bush peonies—and not listed to cultivar. Fortunately for gardeners, the bush peony roots usually work perfectly to supply the tree-peony top with the nutrients and energy it needs to grow. In essence, the bush-peony roots are nurse roots that, if all goes well, will be naturally replaced by tree peony roots. However, if something damages the top, or for whatever reason the bush peony roots grow more vigorously than the top, then new stems can be sent up from the roots. These stems are not the tree peony, they are growth from the unknown bush peony root-stock.

It's not uncommon to see different foliage arising around grafted tree peonies in gardens where the owners are unaware of the problem. To avoid this problem, plant the graft deeply. Deep planting helps keep the rootstock in a roots-only mode and allows the tree peony to root for itself over time. If the bush peony rootstock does send up its own stems, immediately remove them. The stems and leaves will look different in shape, size, and color values from the tree peony leaves.

One option to control this problem is to dig up plants in the fall and look at the roots. If the tree peony part has started to root, cut out most or all of the stocky herbaceous roots, which will look different than narrower and fibrous

Intersectional peonies, such as 'Cora Louise', are appealing landscape plants all season long.

tree peony roots. Replant the tree peony now to establish on its own roots. It is much simpler to start with own-root plants.

Home gardeners interested in grafting should consult manuals on plant propagation as well as the web sites of the American and Canadian Peony Societies for experienced suggestions. Some of the regional peony societies sponsor grafting workshops for members, especially in late summer. There are useful videos on the web, too.

It is exciting to grow your own peony from seed. Gardeners interested in growing peonies from seed will find that they are easy to grow, but will take sometimes more than five years to go from seedling to the first bloom. The American Peony Society has a peony seed distribution program for members. The seeds become available in the fall and each shipment is accompanied by growing instructions. The seeds you receive generally were open pollinated, which means the bees did the crossing, so they will not be the same as the parent, but a totally new peony.

Cut

Flowers

Bountiful Bouquets

Peony bouquets often accent the exceptional days of our lives. What bouquet isn't lifted to another level when peonies are included? Many brides and their mothers sense that peonies in bloom will convey that romantic aura. Graceful, often fragrant, and in the full range from chaste whites through blushing pinks, culminating in boldly festive corals, yellows, and reds of every hue, peonies are suitable for all kinds of celebrations.

As you design your garden with peonies, consider growing other flowers that bloom at the same time. Our list of companion plants is based on decades of experience. Harmonize your garden plantings with the kinds, forms, and colors of flowers that complement your peonies. This way you'll create your own distinctive living treasury of bouquet-ready flowers. These can become signature bouquets that could have come from no other garden but yours. Share them with pride and pleasure.

Cut Flower Care

Simple steps guarantee success. Cut flowers during the cool part of the day. Use clean, sanitized tools and containers. Remove all foliage that will be underwater. Recut the stem underwater just as it is put in the vase. Finally, display in a cool location out of direct sunlight for a longer-lasting bouquet. Now for the details.

Everyone loves peonies in bouquets, whether as single stems, or grouped with other peonies, or mixed with other flowers and foliage. A few tricks can help your cut peonies be superlative. While many home gardeners cut peonies in bloom for use right then, for important events or for sharing peony flowers, it's best to cut the stems in bud and allow the bud to open in the vase.

Cut peony flowers or buds early in the morning while the buds are still cool. Leave at least three sets of leaves on the stem below the cut to keep the plant vigorous. Most varieties can be cut when the bud feels like a large, firm marshmallow or when you observe the first petal move away from the bud. If you feel a hard marble texture when squeezing the bud, the bud is still too tight to cut.

Wait for it to partially open. Each variety can vary in cutting stage. A single bloom must be cut tighter than a double bloom. When a stem is cut with a tight bud, the flower may not open. When learning stages to cut blooms it is helpful to take some buds in the house to observe if and how they open.

Wash and bleach all tools, buckets, and vases to reduce the flower's contact with bacteria. Place the stems immediately in cool water. Remove all foliage that will be below water level in your final arrangement as the foliage will begin to break down under water causing bacteria to begin to grow, giving your flowers a shorter vase life.

Buds of 'Coral Charm' at the correct cutting stage for enjoying long-lasting bouquets.

Fill the sink or a bowl with 3–4 inches (8–10 cm) of cool water, and put the stem and the snips in the water to recut the stem as you are finally placing the bloom in the arrangement. This way the stem end, which may have dried as you were gathering the flowers, is removed. When you lift the stem after cutting it, you will see that a drop of water is clinging to the stem end, thus protecting the tissue that takes up the water. Re-cutting in that manner every two or three days will remove any stem ends that begin to decay in the water.

Keep the flowers out of direct sunlight and away from heat. Change the water in the vases daily, if possible, to reduce bacteria count. In floral arrangements, you might want to use a commercial flower food that contains both sugar to feed the flower and a bacterial inhibitor to keep the water fresh. Flowers should not be put in a refrigerator that also contains fruit as fruit emits ethylene gas that speeds flower maturity.

To hold buds and flowers for a few days, stand them in a container of water in a cool, dark place. The optimum holding temperature is 33°F (1°C); however, refrigerator temperatures will also slow the maturity. Placing a plastic bag loosely over the buds will help retain moisture that would be pulled out by frost-free refrigerators. Allow two or three days for tight buds to open. To hasten opening, place the stems in warm water in a warm place with good light.

Extend your season with bouquets. No one would know these peonies were refrigerated in bud for over a week.

Bush

Peonies

'Alexander Woollcott'

Arthur P. Saunders, 1941
UNITED STATES

Intensely shiny red blooms that retain their color and intensity throughout flower maturity, with incredible purity of red coloration across the two rows of petals. This short plant is outstanding in every respect and one of the most impressive of Saunders's crosses between *P. lactiflora* and *P. peregrina*. A camera can't capture the brilliant, intense color. Dark fire-engine red large flowers will blaze from across your garden. The flowers hold their color well as they mature. Place it at the front of the border for its shorter stature.

KIND Herbaceous hybrid

COLOR Crimson red

FLORAL FORM Semidouble

FRAGRANCE Not noted

SEASON Early midseason

HEIGHT 24 inches (30 cm)

SUPPORT Not needed

NOTE Aptly named after the man who is said to be one of the most charismatic American drama critics and commentators of his or any other time. Alexander Woollcott was one of America's important war reporters and drama critics in the first part of the twentieth century and a famous alumnus of Hamilton College, where peony breeder Arthur P. Saunders was a professor of chemistry. This is one of the great peonies Saunders introduced as Lobata hybrids. It gets its luscious color from the *P. peregrina* parent.

'Amalia Olson'

Christian Olson, 1959
UNITED STATES

Wonderful fragrance tops off the quality list for 'Amalia Olson'. Accolades don't stop there—it was chosen as peony of the year for 2012 by the American Peony Society. The pure white bloom is a dependable opener when the temperatures are hot. Strong stems hold the flower well in wet weather. Blush coloration may show on opening in cool weather, then turn white with maturity. Some reports of pleasing fall leaf color changes.

KIND Lactiflora
COLOR White
FLORAL FORM Double
FRAGRANCE Very fragrant
SEASON Late
HEIGHT 32 inches (81 cm)
SUPPORT Not needed
CUT FLOWER Excellent
NOTE Named after the hybridizer's mother. Donald Hollingsworth praised it as one of the finest peonies for any purpose.

AWARDS APS Gold Medal 2011

'Angel Cheeks'

Carl G. Klehm, 1970
UNITED STATES

The elegant lady of peonies. The clear-pink petals mound atop a narrow band of refined ivory petals above cupped, pink guard petals. It exudes a purity of color and form. Add the lovely scent to know it is aptly named—heavenly, indeed. A slightly shorter plant, begging to be at the front of the flower bed for your enjoyment. 'Angel Cheeks' is great for blending colors in the garden as well as in bouquets.

KIND Lactiflora
COLOR Cameo pink, for overall effect
FLORAL FORM Bomb-type double
FRAGRANCE Very fragrant, especially at twilight
SEASON Midseason
HEIGHT To 32 inches (81 cm)
SUPPORT Not needed

AWARDS APS Award of Landscape Merit;
APS Gold Medal 2005

'Ann Berry Cousins'

Lyman W. Cousins, 1972
CANADA

An unusual salmon-pink bloom that can have varied form on the bush, ranging from single to semidouble. On vigorous plants, there are even blooms that aspire to be double. Large, cupped petals encompass both yellow and self-color in the center, with additional excitement being elicited by the varied appearance of individual blooms. One bloom per stem allows it to grow without support.

KIND Herbaceous hybrid	**SEASON** Early midseason
COLOR Salmon pink	**HEIGHT** To 30 inches (76 cm)
FLORAL FORM Semidouble	**SUPPORT** Not needed
FRAGRANCE Lightly fragrant	

'Ann Cousins'

Lyman W. Cousins, 1946
CANADA

A white mound of gracefully curved petals. It's an almost painful experience, waiting and watching for it to fully open, and then you can't stay away from its perfume. It's not over until 'Ann Cousins' takes charge of your garden and bouquets. The fully double flowers are so large that they will need support, especially if you want them to open in best form.

KIND Lactiflora

COLOR White

FLORAL FORM Double

FRAGRANCE Very fragrant

SEASON Late

HEIGHT 32 inches (81 cm)

SUPPORT Needed

CUT FLOWER Excellent

NOTE One of the last bloomers among the fragrant whites. 'Elsa Sass' is similar but has a slight blush towards the center. Not to be confused with the pink-flowered but almost identically named 'Ann Berry Cousins'.

AWARDS APS Best in Show 1954

'Athena'

Arthur P. Saunders, 1955
UNITED STATES

A rare bloom coloration that is striking, with its raspberry flares radiating from the base of the petals to creamy to white petal edges. The flares are enhanced by curly yellow stamens that themselves are punctuated by raspberry carpel tips in the center of the bloom. A strongly erect plant, with a very early bloom time to hail the opening of the peony season.

KIND Herbaceous hybrid
COLOR Creamy white
FLORAL FORM Single
FRAGRANCE None
SEASON Very early
HEIGHT To 30 inches (76 cm)
SUPPORT Not needed
NOTE This is one of Saunders's prime achievements: producing a cultivar having a pedigree of four different peony species in its parentage.

'Avalanche'

Félix Crousse, 1886
FRANCE

Expect to be swept up with this snowy-white double bloom that's an avalanche of petals, some with red flecks on the edges and a light-yellow glow from the base of the petals. Lightly fragrant and similar to 'Festiva Maxima' but coming later in the season. Good petal texture adds to the flower's substance and it stands up nicely. An heirloom peony that has stood the test of time.

KIND Lactiflora
COLOR White
FLORAL FORM Double
FRAGRANCE Lightly fragrant
SEASON Midseason
HEIGHT 35 inches (89 cm)
SUPPORT Not needed, especially if side buds removed.
CUT FLOWER Excellent
NOTE Alice Harding considered 'Avalanche' to be a "[p]erfectly formed flower."

'Big Ben'

Edward Auten, 1943
UNITED STATES

Held high above the foliage, 'Big Ben' is a bloom to behold. The distinctive fragrance alone will capture you. Carol can always tell she has included it in a bouquet by the wonderful fragrance, rare in red peonies. The color of red is difficult to capture in photos, darker than 'Félix Crousse' but lighter than 'Red Charm', just the right red for this bomb-type bloom. Good performer in hot climates.

KIND Lactiflora
COLOR Red
FLORAL FORM Bomb-type double
FRAGRANCE Very fragrant
SEASON Early midseason
HEIGHT To 36 inches (91 cm)
SUPPORT Likely needed
CUT FLOWER Excellent

'Belleville'

Harold Wolfe / Donald Hollingsworth, 1988
UNITED STATES

Unusual, delightful color contrast of darker guard petals which cup a profusion of spikey striped center petals. Sidebuds prolong the bloom season.

KIND Lactiflora
COLOR Light cyclamen purple
FLORAL FORM Anemone
FRAGRANCE Lightly fragrant
SEASON Midseason
HEIGHT 34 inches (86 cm)
SUPPORT May be needed

'Blaze'

Orville W. Fay, 1973
UNITED STATES

A passionate scarlet to fire engine-red heartthrob. Single flowers are brightest cheerful red, heightened by the wavy petal edges with a golden center of anthers. Leaves are dark green. The whole plant, in bloom, brightens up the season. This strongly growing variety with a sturdy plant habit is somewhat shorter than many, so best placed towards the front of the border.

KIND Herbaceous hybrid

COLOR Red

FLORAL FORM Single

FRAGRANCE Lightly fragrant

SEASON Early midseason

HEIGHT 32 inches (81 cm)

SUPPORT Not needed

NOTE Thought to have an ancestry related to 'Paula Fay', so it is not surprising that both are very bright peonies in the garden.

'Blushing Princess'

David L. Reath, 1991
UNITED STATES

What a princess. A frilly, pale-pink bloom that glows from the red carpel tips in the center. Strong stems carry the flowers well. The few side buds extend the blooming season in the garden (unless they are removed). The foliage is relatively large and dark green, ready to be a verdant workhorse in your garden long after the bloom season is over.

KIND Herbaceous hybrid
COLOR Light pink to white
FLORAL FORM Semidouble
FRAGRANCE Pleasing
SEASON Early
HEIGHT 32 inches (81 cm)
SUPPORT Not needed

'Bouquet Perfect'

Robert Tischler, 1987
UNITED STATES

Aptly named for its stately form, luscious color, and slight fragrance. The larger guard petals are set off by the mound of serrated petals in the center—all held in pleasing symmetry. Great things come in small packages, so put this relatively short peony at the front of your garden bed.

KIND Lactiflora
COLOR Pink
FLORAL FORM Anemone
FRAGRANCE Slightly fragrant
SEASON Midseason
HEIGHT 24 inches (60 cm)
SUPPORT Not needed

'Bowl of Beauty'

Aart Hoogendoorn, 1949
NETHERLANDS

Bright and cheery, large, pink petals cup an unusual center of spiky or fringed creamy petaloids. On occasion, some individual flowers have, almost as an exclamation, a fountain of deep rose petals bursting from the center, as if they were releasing the ever-present fragrance. 'Bowl of Beauty' is not only the name, it is an accolade, describing this simply elegant plant.

KIND Lactiflora

COLOR Pink

FLORAL FORM Anemone

FRAGRANCE Very fragrant

SEASON Midseason

HEIGHT To 32 inches (81 cm)

SUPPORT Usually not needed

AWARDS RHS Award of Garden Merit 1993

'Bowl of Cream'

Carl G. Klehm, 1963
UNITED STATES

The lusciously creamy white petals completely fill the fully formed flower, with golden-yellow anthers nearly hidden among the petals, adding the warm tones. There are reports of individual flowers being 8 inches to more than 9 inches (20–23 cm) across. Strong stems with few side buds make this an excellent garden and cut flower selection.

KIND Lactiflora
COLOR Creamy white
FLORAL FORM Double
FRAGRANCE Lightly fragrant
SEASON Midseason
HEIGHT To 34 inches (86 cm)
SUPPORT Usually not needed
CUT FLOWER Excellent

NOTE In time, this will likely be considered a classic mid-twentieth century introduction, as it has the visual appeal of the best French cultivars from the nineteenth century, its own subtle fragrance, and strong stems that let it be grown in the garden without serious staking. 'Mother's Choice' is more blush-toned.

AWARDS APS Gold Medal 1981; APS Best in Show 1994

'Bridal Shower'

Roy G. Klehm, 1981
UNITED STATES

A glowing heart of yellow shines through the central white petals that mass above the wider guard petals. A graceful and elegant form made even more pleasing by its fragrance. The yellow glow comes from stamens that have been transformed into small yellow petaloids interspersed among the inner petals. Perfect for weddings.

KIND Lactiflora
COLOR White
FLORAL FORM Bomb-type double
FRAGRANCE Fragrant
SEASON Midseason
HEIGHT To 34 inches (86 cm)
SUPPORT May be needed
NOTE One of Klehm's fragrant white peonies.

'Brother Chuck'

Roy G. Klehm, 1995
UNITED STATES

Dignified, fragrant, rose-shaped, double, white blooms with a pink glow towards the center. Pleasing range of petal forms and colors from the outer guards to the central petals. Strong stems carry the flowers well.

KIND Lactiflora
COLOR White to soft blush
FLORAL FORM Double
FRAGRANCE Fragrant
SEASON Midseason
HEIGHT 28 inches (71 cm)
SUPPORT Not needed
NOTE Named by Klehm for his beloved brother Carl "who loved the excitement of the peony conventions and displayed blossoms for so many people to enjoy."

AWARDS APS Best of Show 2008

'Buckeye Belle'

Walter Mains, 1956
UNITED STATES

Exceptionally dark-red, satiny blooms, almost chocolate-red, are sprinkled with golden stamens. The flower form can vary from a fairly open center to tightly packed petals, depending on the vigor of the plant. The blooms are slightly fragrant and stand up well without support. Since 'Buckeye Belle' blooms early and is relatively short, you'll want it near the front of your garden beds or near paths. An added bonus is the striking maroon fall foliage. Truly phenomenal. As a cut flower, it provides a strong and, at times, much needed color.

KIND Herbaceous hybrid
COLOR Extremely dark red, sometimes described as mahogany to maroon
FLORAL FORM Semidouble
FRAGRANCE Lightly fragrant
SEASON Early
HEIGHT To 30 inches (76 cm)
SUPPORT Not needed
CUT FLOWER Excellent
NOTE 'Buckeye Belle' honors Ohio, the Buckeye State, and is too new (1956) for the historic Peony Garden at the University of Michigan's Nichols Arboretum, or the temptation to have this splendid peony referring to an arch-rival institution might have proven too much to resist!

AWARDS APS Award of Landscape Merit; APS Gold Medal 2010

'Candy Heart'

MYRON D. BIGGER, 1961

UNITED STATES

Eye-candy for the peony garden. Large, white petals with light-red streaks and shading are veritable floral peppermint candies just waiting for you and your guests, to sate your appetite. A delightfully different and refreshing flower in gardens and bouquets.

KIND Lactiflora

COLOR White, with pink tints and red stripes

FLORAL FORM Double

FRAGRANCE Fragrant

SEASON Midseason

HEIGHT 34 inches (86 cm)

SUPPORT May be needed

NOTE The pleasing fragrance of this cultivar comes from its seed mother, 'Monsieur Jules Elie'.

'Candy Stripe'

Roger F. Anderson, 1992

UNITED STATES

What fetching eye-candy for the garden or bouquets. 'Candy Stripe' looks good enough to pop in your mouth and savor. Double, white blooms are pleasantly streaked with red—and some petals are suffused with a tinge of pink—and are fragrant. It's impossible not to think of peppermint candies. Vigorous plants that might only be perfected if they had a peppermint aroma.

KIND Lactiflora

COLOR Bicolored, white with red stripes and some pink tones

FLORAL FORM Double

FRAGRANCE Mild

SEASON Mid to late

HEIGHT To 36 inches (91 cm)

SUPPORT May be needed, especially on the longer stems

CUT FLOWER Stunning

'Carnation Bouquet'

William Seidl, 1996
UNITED STATES

Perfectly named both for the flower form and for the spicy fragrance. The appealing pink color lightens on the petal tips but is deeper pink in the depth of the bloom. A full double with petals that are ruffled on the edges and all the same size. The foliage has a more rounded shape than most peonies.

KIND Herbaceous hybrid
COLOR Pink
FLORAL FORM Double
FRAGRANCE Very fragrant
SEASON Midseason
HEIGHT To 32 inches (81 cm)
SUPPORT Needed

'Chestine Gowdy'

Oliver F. Brand / Archie M. Brand, 1913
UNITED STATES

Romantically fragrant puffs of creamy pink and white blooms stun garden visitors and have done so since 1913. The striking two-toned flowers are pinkest through the inner and outer petals, separated by creamy elegance. There may be a few red edgings on the inner petals. A very Victorian pastel effect enhanced with a rose scent.

KIND Lactiflora
COLOR Pink
FLORAL FORM Double
FRAGRANCE Very fragrant
SEASON Late midseason
HEIGHT To 34 inches (86 cm)
SUPPORT Needed
NOTE 'Chestine Gowdy' is Brand's salute to an inspiring teacher who led a one-room school house. Dr. Upjohn praised it as "very attractive." A great peony and quite the living tribute.

'Chocolate Soldier'

Edward Auten, 1939
UNITED STATES

The peony for chocoholics, at least for the intensely saturated chocolate-red color that is stunningly set off by the yellow anthers and red carpels. Your garden guests, once over the sensational color, may note occasional flowers are double rather than Japanese, and some flowers may have yellow flecks on the central petals. All variations are sensational. A classic that is worth the effort to find.

KIND Herbaceous hybrid
COLOR Dark reddish brown to maroon
FLORAL FORM Japanese to double (variable)
FRAGRANCE None
SEASON Midseason
HEIGHT 28 inches (71 cm)
SUPPORT Not needed

NOTE This is one of Auten's few surviving cultivars that reflects Africa-American contributions to American culture, chocolate soldier being then a contemporary term for enlisted African-American men. The name is a double-entendre. Either way, this selection is strong, handsome, and distinctive. It is one of David's favorite peonies of all time.

'Christmas Velvet'

Roger F. Anderson, 1992
UNITED STATES

Christmas in peony season. Velvet-red flowers are intensely petal-packed, almost stacked up one upon the other as gifts beneath the Christmas tree. A tight, bright-red bloom with full flowers that have a distinctive elegance. Strong stems hold the flowers well, in the garden and in bouquets.

KIND Herbaceous hybrid
COLOR Red
FLORAL FORM Double
FRAGRANCE Fragrant

SEASON Midseason
HEIGHT To 30 inches (76 cm)
SUPPORT Not needed

'Color Magnet'

Donald Hollingsworth, 1994
UNITED STATES

A bright color highlighted by a golden-yellow boss of stamens. Attracts attention in the garden. Blooms, which are cupped when young and then open widely, are reported to be relatively redder during a cool bloom seas. Stands up nicely without support.

KIND Herbaceous hybrid
COLOR Bright violet-pink
FLORAL FORM Single
FRAGRANCE None
SEASON Midseason
HEIGHT 32 inches (81 cm)
SUPPORT Not needed

'Comanche'

Myron D. Bigger, 1957
UNITED STATES

Vivid-magenta petals encompass a shredded center of magenta to yellow that fades even lighter. A definitely eye-catching and unusual form, bound to be a conversation piece in your garden. The blooms are held just high enough above the dark-green foliage for a good show. The flower form allows water to drain easily to keep the bloom upright.

KIND Lactiflora
COLOR Magenta pink
FLORAL FORM Japanese
FRAGRANCE Lightly fragrant
SEASON Midseason
HEIGHT To 36 inches (91 cm)
SUPPORT Not needed

AWARDS APS Award of Landscape Merit

'Cora Stubbs'

William H. Krekler, 1976
UNITED STATES

Feast your eyes and then inhale the perfume that floats out of the creamy white center poised on large raspberry-pink petals. Nature blended the color tones perfectly. Many side buds allow for an extended season. 'Cora Stubbs' is technically a Japanese form, but well-developed flowers evoke the bomb form in fullness, and in the original meaning of an ice cream dessert. Yum!

KIND Lactiflora

COLOR Pink

FLORAL FORM Anemone

FRAGRANCE Very fragrant

SEASON Midseason

HEIGHT 32 inches (81 cm)

SUPPORT Usually not needed

'Coral Charm'

Samuel E. Wissing, 1964
CANADA

Coral-toned flowers on very vigorous plants. The large, cup-shaped flowers feature a central mass of golden-yellow stamens. The flowers open an exotic, deep, and brilliant coral that fades to include softer, yellower tones after opening. In the garden during peak bloom, color tones representing all stages of flowering can be present, making for a display that will stop you in your tracks. This back-of-the-border plant usually needs staking.

KIND Herbaceous hybrid

COLOR Coral, with peach to apricot tones

FLORAL FORM Semidouble

FRAGRANCE Lightly fragrance, not always pleasant to all noses

SEASON Early midseason

HEIGHT To 40 inches (102 cm) or taller

SUPPORT Needed

CUT FLOWER Excellent

NOTE 'Coral Charm' was the very first of the coral colors. If you're enchanted by coral tones in peonies, consider three leading contenders. 'Coral Sunset' differs from 'Coral Charm' in the range of coral colors, including lighter yellow tones as the flower matures, and in having very strong stems. 'Coral 'n Gold' has color tones that range to golden yellow. All look stunning with blue-toned flowers either in the garden or in a floral arrangement.

AWARDS APS Gold Medal 1986; APS Best in Show 2003, 2006; RHS Award of Garden Merit 2012

'Coral Sunset'

Samuel E. Wissing / Charles Klehm & Son Nursery, 1981
UNITED STATES

The most spectacular coral flower, so far, in the realm of peonies. This vigorous plant has intense, deep coral flowers that
mature to an elegant ivory. The changing color tones flow so
well that it is a delight to behold in its metamorphoses. Would
that even a handful of summer sunsets were equal to this
peony's bloom. The petals have ruffled edges that increase
the flower fullness. Holding its flowers closer to the foliage than
'Coral Charm' helps it to stand more upright. Usually there is
only one bud per stem, but sometimes a side bud appears.

KIND Herbaceous hybrid

COLOR Coral

FLORAL FORM Semidouble

FRAGRANCE Slightly fragrant,
not always pleasant

SEASON Early

HEIGHT To 36 inches (91 cm)

SUPPORT Not needed

CUT FLOWER Excellent

NOTE By any measure, 'Coral
Sunset' sets the standard for coral
tones in modern peonies. The
depth of color leaves no doubt
in our minds that this will be
regarded as one of the important
bush peonies introduced in the
last quarter of the twentieth
century. Roy Klehm noted this as
his favorite coral-colored peony.
Thought to be closely related to
'Coral Charm'.

AWARDS APS Award of Landscape Merit; APS Gold Medal 2003

'Coral 'n Gold'

Lyman W. Cousins / Roy G. Klehm, 1981
CANADA / UNITED STATES

The floral cup of 'Coral 'n Gold' is an appealing, deep-toned coral that embraces the lively congregation of golden stamens. The overall effect is as if vibrant poppies decided they wanted to become peonies, in the best way possible. The distinctive coral tone has been described as rose coral, apricot coral, or soft coral, but we find that peach coral captures the sense of its complex hues. The floral form is single, even though there may be two overlapping rows of guard petals.

KIND Herbaceous hybrid

COLOR Peach coral, even with nearly orange values

FLORAL FORM Single

FRAGRANCE Slightly sweet to none

SEASON Midseason

HEIGHT To 34 inches (86 cm)

SUPPORT Not needed

NOTE Lyman W. Cousins of Ontario included this in his Innerglow line of stunning hybrid peonies.

AWARDS APS Award of Landscape Merit

'Cream Puff'

Walter Marx, 1981
UNITED STATES

It should be named 'Touched by a Fairy' as it is so delightful and delicate in appearance. The lacy center glows in a profusion of yellow and pink.

KIND Lactiflora

COLOR Very light pink

FLORAL FORM Japanese

FRAGRANCE Lightly fragrant

SEASON Midseason

HEIGHT 36 inches (91 cm)

SUPPORT Not needed

'Cytherea'

Arthur P. Saunders, 1953
UNITED STATES

The brilliant cherry-rose bloom attracts the eye immediately in the garden, since its cupped shape approaches perfection. The same color shows in the carpel tips, surrounded by golden stamens. The bloom eventually fades to a paler pink. Throughout the flower's life, it displays unusual and sought-after color tones. 'Cytherea' is a shorter plant that holds the blooms close to the foliage and without support. Use it near the front of the border.

KIND Herbaceous hybrid
COLOR Deep rose
FLORAL FORM Semidouble
FRAGRANCE Slight to none
SEASON Early
HEIGHT 24 inches (60 cm)
SUPPORT Not needed

NOTE This is one of Saunders's most famous Lobata hybrids, a group of technically challenging hybrids developed through the then-named *P. lobata* to bring clear, bright colors to the herbaceous peonies. Classic selections like 'Cytherea' are still pinnacles of excellence and will likely remain popular for generations for their unusually toned flowers.

AWARDS APS Award of Landscape Merit; APS Gold Medal 1980; APS Best in Show 1970, 1976, 1983

'Do Tell'

Edward Auten, 1946
UNITED STATES

A breathtaking peony. A bold confection of multicolor and shredded staminodes erupts from the center of the pale-pink outer petals, which appear as though brushed on by an artist. The delightful, multicolored, twisty center brings a vibrant excitement to the pastel bloom. Flowers are held on the strong stems of tidy plants. A one-of-a-kind peony.

KIND Lactiflora

COLOR Orchid pink

FLORAL FORM Japanese

FRAGRANCE Nearly none

SEASON Midseason

HEIGHT 32 inches (81 cm)

SUPPORT Not needed

NOTE 'Do Tell' is one of Auten's most striking Japanese introductions and reflects a clear aesthetic change from most of the Japanese cultivars available in North American up to that time. The varied pink colors of the fantastically flared staminodes, aptly described as shredded coconut, contrast beautifully with the pale orchid-pink outer petals. The overall effect is stunning and beautiful. The wry humor of the name itself, 'Do Tell', appeals to David, who fell in love with this selection the moment he saw it blooming in the Peony Garden of the Nichols Arboretum.

AWARDS APS Award of Landscape Merit; APS Gold Medal 2004

'Doreen'

Henry E. Sass, 1949
UNITED STATES

'Doreen' stands out, but it takes a moment to appreciate how it does this. Magenta-rose to light pink petals surround a mass of delightfully frilly, golden petaloids, creating an eye-catching flower. If you're seeking striking pinks, 'Doreen is a "wow" for you. Strong stems hold the blooms well. The open flower form allows it to stand up well in harsh weather.

KIND Lactiflora
COLOR Magenta-rose
FLORAL FORM Japanese
FRAGRANCE Lightly fragrant
SEASON Midseason
HEIGHT 32 inches (81 cm)
SUPPORT Not needed

'Dr. F. G. Brethour'

Hans P. Sass, 1938
UNITED STATES

Pure, romantically fluffy white flowers with a creamy glow from within radiate a sense of purity. Huge, many-petaled blooms waft fragrance. Flowering stems have an occasional side bud.

KIND Lactiflora
COLOR White
FLORAL FORM Double
FRAGRANCE Fragrant
SEASON Late
HEIGHT To 34 inches (86 cm)
SUPPORT May be needed

'Duchess de Nemours'

Jacques Calot, 1856
FRANCE

The globe-shaped, creamy white flower is subtly enhanced
by the yellow glow coming from the base of the central petals.
The green carpels add the perfect color note. The Duchess is
known for the purity of its white color. Although not a bright
white, it has no red, pink, or blush tones in the flower or bud.
The medium-size flower is also good for floral arrangements
that are not of palace-size scale. Always stunning in bloom,
with a heady fragrance that is easily appreciated after morning
twilight. The stems may need staking for the best display or
cut flowers. A much-loved old favorite, for generations.

KIND Lactiflora

COLOR Creamy white

FLORAL FORM Double

FRAGRANCE Very fragrant, the way peonies should be

SEASON Midseason

HEIGHT To 34 inches (86 cm)

SUPPORT Usually not needed

CUT FLOWER Excellent

NOTE 'Duchess de Nemours' must have been a sensation when it was
introduced, not only for the fully double flowers, but also for the heady
fragrance that carries so well across the garden or a room that it graces
in a bouquet. For a classic fragrance combination, it pairs well for aroma
and color with 'Monsieur Jules Elie'. Alice Harding lauds this selection
with one word—"exquisite." Dr. Upjohn wryly appreciated 'Duchesse de
Nemours' during Prohibition, when the sale of any alcoholic beverage
was illegal in the United States. He penned, "While its appearance is
most pleasing, its fragrance is said to be 'most intoxicating'. This
should make it the popular peony in dry America." It still is.

AWARDS RHS Award of Garden Merit 1993

'Earlybird'

Arthur P. Saunders, 1951
UNITED STATES

Simply the cutest little flower that greets you with its sunny red face. The fine lacy foliage is a pleasing contrast with other garden foliage. This is a strain, rather than a clone, so there may be slight variation among individual plants.

KIND Herbaceous hybrid
COLOR Red
FLORAL FORM Single
FRAGRANCE Not noted
SEASON Very early
HEIGHT 20 inches (51 cm)
SUPPORT Not needed

'Edulis Superba'

Nicholas Lemon, 1824
FRANCE

Fluffy, bright pink, and fragrant all describe 'Edulis Superba'. In style for almost one hundred and fifty years, it is still a vivacious dowager among herbaceous peonies. It has a slightly smaller bloom on plants that put out a multitude of stems. The result is an abundance of flowers. Side buds add to the number of blooms and length of bloom, but if they're removed, the central flower will be larger than if side buds are left on. Always present are ivory petals just above the guard petals. This selection hasn't been out of fashion for nearly two centuries. It has rightfully earned and retains a firm hold, across generations, on our hearts, as well as a place in our gardens and certainly in bouquets, especially when a medium-sized bloom is needed. Even by the early twentieth century, this was regarded as a tried-and-true variety, with the bonus of delightful fragrance, sometimes described as the essence of classic roses.

KIND Lactiflora

COLOR Pink

FLORAL FORM Double

FRAGRANCE Fragrant to very fragrant

SEASON Midseason

HEIGHT To 36 inches (91 cm)

SUPPORT Needed

CUT FLOWER Excellent

NOTE 'Edulis Superba' may be still available where peonies are locally grown for the farm and florist markets. Early in the twentieth century, Alice Harding recorded that it was already "an old garden favorite because of its fragrance and earliness." Dr. Upjohn appreciated it for blooming consistently on time for Memorial Day decorations (late May) in southwestern Michigan: "Few others have this distinction." The practice of honoring ancestral and military graves with peony bouquets, and sometimes the plant itself, as a living memorial, has been nearly lost in the ensuing century. This grande dame retains a deep and intriguing mystery; she is likely very close to a currently unrecognized but perhaps still extant ornamental herbaceous peony in China. DNA fingerprinting will help resolve by what name she, or her parents, came to Western Europe so long ago.

'Eliza Lundy'

William H. Krekler, 1975
UNITED STATES

A glowing, cranberry-red bloom, with the guard petals holding the center petals as a bouquet in itself. A compact plant for the front of the border. The flower nods, although the bloom is of moderate size.

KIND Herbaceous hybrid

COLOR Red

FLORAL FORM Bomb-type double

FRAGRANCE None

SEASON Early

HEIGHT To 24 inches (60 cm)

SUPPORT Not needed

AWARDS APS Award of Landscape Merit; APS Gold Medal 2016

'Elsa Sass'

Hans P. Sass, 1930
UNITED STATES

An elegant, white double to finish the peony season. The large, velvety petals are perfectly arranged to create a rose-type bloom. The plant is short and compact, with dark-green leaves and strong stems, so consider the front of the border, to best enjoy the pleasant fragrance of the last-of-peony bloom season. Yes, it's late, but worth every moment. Definitely a case of saving the best for last.

KIND Lactiflora

COLOR White

FLORAL FORM Double rose-form

FRAGRANCE Very fragrant

SEASON Late

HEIGHT To 28 inches (71 cm)

SUPPORT Not needed

NOTE Much of the breeding work in North American in the early- to mid-twentieth century aimed at extending the range of colors and the bloom period; peonies that bloomed earlier were keenly appreciated. Since the wild *P. lactiflora* is inherently among the last-blooming of the common species, the hybrids with other species tend to bloom even earlier. By contrast, 'Elsa Sass' is an otherwise traditional and fragrant selection that pushes the season to the very end, to the delight of gardeners and florists.

AWARDS APS Gold Medal 1943

'Etched Salmon'

Lyman W. Cousins / Roy G. Klehm, 1981
CANADA / **UNITED STATES**

Can it be real? The salmon pink is darker at the base of the bloom, lightening slightly, with shadows of mystery in its depths. Maybe it is just a painting hiding in the garden! The foliage encloses the bloom like an Elizabethan collar. Irresistible. One of the few peonies to win so many major awards, so quickly.

KIND Herbaceous hybrid

COLOR Pink

FLORAL FORM Double

FRAGRANCE Fragrant

SEASON Midseason

HEIGHT To 34 inches (86 cm)

SUPPORT Not needed

AWARDS APS Award of Landscape Merit; APS Gold Medal 2002; APS Best in Show 1990

'Fairy Princess'

Lyman D. Glasscock / Elizabeth Falk, 1955
UNITED STATES

With a pixie cuteness, 'Fairy Princess' is a tidy, compact, dwarf plant that holds its clear red blooms cheerfully face-up to greet you on the garden border. A hybrid variety of uncertain parentage, it is well worth having for the garden border or the rock garden.

KIND Herbaceous hybrid

COLOR Red

FLORAL FORM Single

FRAGRANCE None

SEASON Early midseason

HEIGHT To 20 inches (51 cm)

SUPPORT Not needed

'Felix Supreme'

Nicholas Kriek, 1955
UNITED STATES

Ruby-red, double flowers have a frothy appearance attribut-able to the many petals. This is a red without the blue tones that previous red Lactiflora peonies tended to show in their coloration. Compared to truly dark red flowers, as in a vase, it sometimes is called dark pink. 'Felix Supreme' holds its color well through maturity, and the color contrasts nicely with the dark green foliage. Some support is required for the best floral dis-plays and cut flowers, as the stems aren't reliably up to the task.

KIND Lactiflora
COLOR Ruby red
FLORAL FORM Double
FRAGRANCE Lightly fragrant
SEASON Midseason
HEIGHT 34 inches (86 cm)
SUPPORT Needed
CUT FLOWER Excellent
NOTE 'Felix Supreme' was one of the important selections introduced by the regionally famous and long-lost Cottage Gardens of Lansing, Michigan. 'Félix Crousse' is of the same color tone, but with a bomb-type bloom. Both are reliable. Try both, and if you strongly prefer one, keep your choice and give the other to a friend, who will undoubtedly be delighted.

'Festiva Maxima'

Auguste Miellez, 1851
FRANCE

This massive, loose, rose-form flower is pure white and lightly flecked with crimson, especially on the petal-edges near the center of the flower. As the flower ages, the petal-ball becomes relaxed and fuller. Mature plants are very floriferous and need staking; even though the stems are strong, the enormous flowers are just too much for the stems in wind and rain. Enjoy the heady fragrance wafting in the garden in early to midmorning. It's the fragrance of memories of old-fashioned gardens, but emanating from a thoroughly time-proven selection worthy of almost every garden today. This peony's sterling qualities of growth, color, and fragrance make it most desirable, even after more than a century and a half.

KIND Lactiflora

COLOR White

FLORAL FORM Double

FRAGRANCE Very fragrant

SEASON Early midseason

HEIGHT To 36 inches (91 cm)

SUPPORT Needed

CUT FLOWER Excellent

NOTE 'Festiva Maxima' remains one of the most popular of the mid-nineteenth century French hybrid peonies, never out of fashion. It is a standard-bearer that helps define classic peonies. Alice Harding noted it bears a "[f]inely formed flower of large, white petals. . . . have grown 'Festiva Maxima' in my garden, with blooms 9 inches across." Dr. Upjohn embraced 'Festiva Maxima' with a delightfully homey note: "Like old furniture, old flowers are kept in fashion because they are good, not because they are old," and then extolled the selection as having "virtues beyond most." Nearly a century later, we agree.

AWARDS RHS Award of Garden Merit 1993

'Garden Lace'

Donald Hollingsworth, 1992
UNITED STATES

Soft-pink, luminous petals cup a tight center of lacy, soft-yellow staminodes. The flower opens wider and the center becomes fluffier as the flower matures and lightens in color. A row of 'Garden Lace' plants, there-fore, can have a delightful array of shades to behold. No support needed. A good landscape plant.

KIND Herbaceous hybrid

COLOR Pink

FLORAL FORM Japanese

FRAGRANCE Lightly fragrant

SEASON Midseason

HEIGHT To 30 inches (76 cm)

SUPPORT Not needed

NOTE Hollingsworth noted that this is one of the most rainproof peonies in the garden. It stands up well to inclement weather.

AWARDS APS Award of Landscape Merit

'Garden Peace'

Arthur P. Saunders, 1941
UNITED STATES

Stunningly elegant white flowers are highlighted by the central boss of golden stamens on crimson-red fila-ments. Red-tinged sepals and stems add to the sense of color on the plant. The several side blooms let 'Garden Peace' begin blooming early and continue flowering right into the peak of peony season. Taller stems may need staking. Destined to be a classic.

KIND Herbaceous hybrid

COLOR White

FLORAL FORM Single

FRAGRANCE None

SEASON Early midseason

HEIGHT To 36 inches (91 cm)

SUPPORT May be needed

NOTE This is one of Saunders's complex hybrids where the side buds are intentional. This way, each stem and the bush overall, have a good show of blossoms.

'Gardenia'

Eugene Lins, 1955
UNITED STATES

Blush to white flowers have a lovely gardenia form of rounded fullness. The center of yellow stamens doesn't appear until the flower is quite mature and then contributes a yellow glow to the bloom. In this peony, weather makes a difference. Blush coloration appears when weather is cloudy at bloom, but sunny conditions cause a white bloom. The fragrance adds another pleasure point. The unopened bud may have a few red streaks that are not visible once the bloom opens.

KIND Lactiflora

COLOR Blush white

FLORAL FORM Double

FRAGRANCE Lightly fragrant

SEASON Midseason

HEIGHT 34 inches (86 cm)

SUPPORT Usually not needed

CUT FLOWER Fine

NOTE 'Gardenia' has won many regional floral show awards. It's meritorious.

'Gay Paree'

Edward Auten, 1933
UNITED STATES

Perfectly named. The bold, cherry-pink guard petals lovingly cup a mound of petaloids, which begin in varying shades of pink and mature to white, an irresistibly cheery color combination. No staking is required for this Japanese-form flower. A grouping takes the breath away, but consider placing single plants throughout the garden to draw your eye from place to place. Otherwise, you might wear out the grass in front of the group while staring in awe. When introduced, this color and form were considered quite the novelty, inspiring accolades like ethereal, fine, and outstanding. It has retained a strong following ever since.

KIND Lactiflora

COLOR Cerise pink

FLORAL FORM Japanese

FRAGRANCE Lightly to moderately fragrant

SEASON Midseason

HEIGHT To 33 inches (84 cm)

SUPPORT Not needed

CUT FLOWER Excellent

AWARDS APS Award of Landscape Merit

'Goldilocks'

Ben Gilbertson, 1975
UNITED STATES

Gorgeous, pale- to clear-yellow blooms float above the bushes and grab everyone's attention. The swirling, yet partially translucent petaloids are a visual treat far more so than the porridge of the namesake Goldilocks and the three bears. As the plant matures, the flower form becomes a bomb-type double. One of the noteworthy yellow bush peonies before the commercial development of intersectional peonies.

KIND Herbaceous hybrid
COLOR Yellow
FLORAL FORM Anemone (younger plants) to bomb-type double (mature plants)
FRAGRANCE Fragrant
SEASON Late midseason
HEIGHT 28 inches (71 cm)
SUPPORT Not needed

'Henry Bockstoce'

William S. Bockstoce, 1955
UNITED STATES

Deep cardinal-red petals give 'Henry Bockstoce' much substance. The satiny sheen across the massive flowers draws the eye and causes visitors to actually walk into the flower bed, even when this tall peony is planted in the back. The double flowers unfold beautifully from the buds, releasing their fragrance. Coming closer, to inhale the perfume, you may notice that some petals are edged with white. The flowers are held well above the foliage, making the plant dramatic in the garden.

KIND Herbaceous hybrid
COLOR Rich cardinal red
FLORAL FORM Double rose-form
FRAGRANCE Fragrant
SEASON Early midseason
HEIGHT 40 inches (102 cm)
SUPPORT Needed
NOTE Although 'Henry Bockstoce' blooms into the mid-season, it is considered one the last of the intense cardinal-red hybrids in the peony parade. If this color range is important to you, consider including 'Old Faithful' as well as 'Henry Bockstoce'.

'Henry Sass'

Hans P. Sass / Interstate Nurseries, 1949
UNITED STATES

A magnificently full, white, double flower that is lightly fragrant. 'Henry Sass' is dependable and consistent. In cloudy, overcast weather the bloom will develop as a blush color. Long flower stems, although strong, do not support the large bloom without staking. 'Henry Sass' mixes well with any of the pink peonies, classic or modern, in the garden as well as in arrangements.

KIND Lactiflora
COLOR White
FLORAL FORM Double
FRAGRANCE Lightly fragrant
SEASON Midseason (to late)
HEIGHT 34 inches (86 cm)
SUPPORT Needed
NOTE One of Sass's mid-century classics that remains popular. The overall effect recalls French peonies of the nineteenth century. Sass introduced many fine peonies that are far from new and not yet old enough to have their revival.

'Hermione'

Hans P. Sass, 1932
UNITED STATES

An old-fashioned delight. Huge flowers with frilly petals that are a rich apple-blossom pink and have a heavenly fragrance.

KIND Lactiflora
COLOR Pink
FLORAL FORM Double
FRAGRANCE Very fragrant
SEASON Late to midseason
HEIGHT 32 inches (81 cm)
SUPPORT May be needed

'Honor'

Arthur P. Saunders, 1941
UNITED STATES

Vibrant color—a bright pink leaning to lavender—makes this peony stand out in the garden. The abundant blooms begin in a cup shape, exposing a center which lightens to a milky hue, drawing you to its lush contrast. So perfect, it can hold you in the garden just to gaze at it.

KIND Herbaceous hybrid
COLOR Bright pink
FLORAL FORM Single (occasionally to semidouble)
FRAGRANCE Lightly fragrant
SEASON Midseason
HEIGHT 36 inches (91 cm)
SUPPORT Usually not needed

'Jan van Leeuwen'

Leonard van Leeuwen, 1928
NETHERLANDS

Subtle, elegant simplicity. Pure-white petals are often notched, making the Japanese flower form appear nearly double. Slightly twisted, yellow staminodes are the same color as the carpel tips. The overall bloom appears as a balance of boldness and delicacy. Strong stems don't need staking.

KIND Lactiflora
COLOR White
FLORAL FORM Japanese
FRAGRANCE Slightly fragrant
SEASON Late
HEIGHT 32 inches (81 cm)
SUPPORT Not needed

'Jean Ericksen'

Jean Ericksen / Marvin Joslin, 1999
CANADA

Feathery red blooms abundantly adorn this bush peony, which draws visitors into the garden with its bold but delicate statement.

KIND Lactiflora

COLOR Deep red

FLORAL FORM Japanese

FRAGRANCE Not noted

SEASON Midseason

HEIGHT To 38 inches (97 cm)

SUPPORT Not needed

NOTE Named by Joslin in honor of Jean Ericksen, of Saskatchewan, who was a noted breeder of award-winning lilies winter-hardy for the Canadian prairies.

'Joker'

Henry Landis / Allan Rogers, 2004
UNITED STATES

The frilly picotee edging appears upon maturity. The bloom begins deep pink with the inner petals becoming lighter with age. A handsome plant in the landscape. Exciting to watch it transform.

KIND Herbaceous hybrid

COLOR Pink, matures white

FLORAL FORM Double

FRAGRANCE Not noted

SEASON Midseason

HEIGHT 32 inches (81 cm)

SUPPORT Not needed

NOTE Landis received this plant as a seedling from William S. Bockstoce.

'Kansas'

Myron D. Bigger, 1940
UNITED STATES

A watermelon-red, voluptuous bloom with consistent symmetry. This enticing red resists fading with maturity. The scalloped inner petal edges add fullness and depth. Strong, reddish stems enhance the visual experience and hold the bloom sturdily. The foliage is clean and dark green. A dependable and enticing cornerstone in the garden, but not quite tall enough for the back of border.

KIND Lactiflora

COLOR Red, and holds well against fading over time

FLORAL FORM Double

FRAGRANCE None to slightly fragrant

SEASON Early midseason

HEIGHT To 36 inches (91 cm)

SUPPORT Not needed

NOTE 'Kansas' was recognized by the editors of the *American Home Magazine* with their American Home Achievement Medal in 1942.

AWARDS APS Gold Medal 1957

'Karl Rosenfield'

Karl Rosenfield, 1908
UNITED STATES

A mainstay. Crimson-red, full bloom that holds glowing golden stamens within its petals. The merry tousle of petals provides a pleasing volume to the bloom. Stems may need help to support the flowers. For authenticity, beware of imposters: it is easy to say that since the flower is red and double, it must be 'Karl Rosenfield'. Adelman's Peony Paradise offers the true variety, dug from the yard of Rosenfield's granddaughter.

KIND Lactiflora

COLOR Red to crimson, sometimes described as bright crimson

FLORAL FORM Double

FRAGRANCE None

SEASON Midseason

HEIGHT To 36 inches (91 cm)

SUPPORT Needed

NOTE This is an easily recognized, old-fashioned peony once you've seen it. Both Dr. Upjohn and Alice Harding appreciated it. Harding lauded it as '[o]ne of the very best reds." Upjohn considered it one of the two best reds (the other is the much less frequently seen 'Ricard Carvel'). Upjohn also appreciated it as a "'good divider." By that he meant the thrifty home gardener or florist could purchase several plants, and within a few years have many more. David has a special place in his heart for 'Karl Rosenfield' as it brings bold red color tones into the Peony Garden of the Nichols Arboretum. In Japan, 'Karl Rosenfield' is known as 'Beni-shinano'.

'Krinkled White'

Archie M. Brand, 1928
UNITED STATES

Purity of the white color of the broad petals sets this variety in a class of its own. Waving in the breeze with a glowing sunshine center of stamens, 'Krinkled White' makes a real statement. It is especially striking in groupings, since the plants produce a nice quantity of blooms. In the garden, the strong stems allow this peony to stand up in rain. It is also considered one of the more drought-tolerant peonies. Absolutely spectacular however used in the garden. It makes a solid bush form.

KIND Lactiflora

COLOR Pure white

FLORAL FORM Single

FRAGRANCE None

SEASON Midseason

HEIGHT To 34 inches (86 cm)

SUPPORT Not needed

NOTE No other single white peony has stood the test of time so well. In 2016, it remains one of the peonies you can find in most public peony gardens, too, since it is the standard by which all other single whites are evaluated, and with good reason, it's close to perfection. Perhaps its only flaw is its absence of fragrance.

AWARDS APS Gold Medal 2008

'La Perle'

Félix Crousse, 1886
FRANCE

A treasured, dainty beauty of a garden jewel. Light rose-pink guard petals surround and embrace the darker inner petals that may be flecked with red. Dreamy, spicy fragrance adds to the antique allure. Always a public favorite at the Peony Garden of the Nichols Arboretum.

KIND Lactiflora

COLOR Lilac-white

FLORAL FORM Double

FRAGRANCE Fragrant

SEASON Midseason

HEIGHT 33 inches (84 cm)

SUPPORT Needed

NOTE Dr. Upjohn felt that "shell pink" best described the complexly light color. "Strong grower . . . . Not disappointing."

'Laura Dessert'

Auguste Dessert, 1913
FRANCE

The glow of sunshine emanates from this century-old beauty. The sturdy, upright plant holds a number of fragrant blooms. The fringed yellow center petals lighten with age. A classic.

KIND Lactiflora

COLOR Pink to white

FLORAL FORM Anemone to double

FRAGRANCE Lightly fragrant

SEASON Early midseason

HEIGHT To 36 inches (91 cm)

SUPPORT May be needed

NOTE A century ago, this was one of the better bush peonies with yellow tones. Dr. Upjohn appreciated what he called canary-yellow tones, but noted suppliers were "scarce."

AWARDS RHS Award of Garden Merit 1993

'Le Cygne'

Lemoine Nursery, 1907
FRANCE

The graceful white swan emerges from a less-than-elegant bud. Patience is required during the stunning transformation to the fragrant, gossamer, classic flower beloved for over a century.

KIND Lactiflora
COLOR White
FLORAL FORM Double
FRAGRANCE Moderately fragrant
SEASON Midseason
HEIGHT 34 inches (86 cm)
SUPPORT May be needed
NOTE This has long been considered one of the best fragrant white peonies—and indeed it's a swan (its name in French). Alice Harding hailed it as one of the best "rare and exquisite peonies" while Dr. Upjohn praised its "great beauty."

AWARDS APS Best in Show 1926, 1956, 1960

'Lemon Chiffon'

David L. Reath, 1981
UNITED STATES

Envision the color of a pale lemon, somehow ruffled into the petals of a peony: 'Lemon Chiffon' delivers exactly what the name promises. The pale but warm-yellow flowers have golden stamens peeking through the center, accenting the raspberry-colored carpel tips. The pleasantly fragrant flowers begin as semidouble, but increase in petal numbers for the first three years. Strong stems hold the flower upright without support.

KIND Herbaceous hybrid
COLOR Yellow
FLORAL FORM Semidouble to bomb
FRAGRANCE Fragrant
SEASON Early
HEIGHT 28 inches (71 cm)
SUPPORT Not needed
NOTE Not only is 'Lemon Chiffon' a stunning yellow hybrid peony, but it is highly fertile. No doubt it will be in the parentage of distinguished cultivars in the future.

AWARDS APS Best in Show 2000

'Little Red Gem'

David L. Reath, 1988
UNITED STATES

The name is a perfect description for this peony. A diminutive gem of filigreed foliage, far different from most peonies. As it prepares to bloom, feathery green balls sprouting delicate light-red blooms appear. A delight to watch emerging in the spring. A rock garden or front border plant.

KIND Herbaceous hybrid
COLOR Red
FLORAL FORM Single
FRAGRANCE Not noted
SEASON Very early
HEIGHT To 18 inches (46 cm)
SUPPORT Not needed

AWARDS APS Award of Landscape Merit

'Lois' Choice'

Chris Laning, 1993
UNITED STATES

Fluffy pink-and-yellow blooms will get even the shy neighbors over for a look. Fascinating color variation across each flower ranges from light pink to yellow and then back to a slightly darker pink. The pinks are warm and the yellows bright. There is absolutely nothing like this!

KIND Herbaceous hybrid
COLOR Multilayered pinks and yellows
FLORAL FORM Double
FRAGRANCE None
SEASON Early
HEIGHT 30 inches (76 cm)
SUPPORT Not needed
NOTE Some imperfections but worth the full circus of coloration.

'Lorelei'

Donald Hollingsworth, 1996
UNITED STATES

Orange with a little pink are the blooms of 'Lorelei' with delightful fading as the bloom matures. As the plant ages, the blooms become fuller. The spicy fragrance is an additional perk.

KIND Herbaceous hybrid

COLOR Orange-pink

FLORAL FORM Bomb-type double

FRAGRANCE Sweet to spicy fragrance

SEASON Midseason

HEIGHT 26 inches (66 cm)

SUPPORT Not needed

NOTE The original Lorelei of German folklore bewitched men with her singing and presence. Let this 'Lorelei' bewitch your garden guests.

'Lovely Rose'

Arthur P. Saunders, 1942
UNITED STATES

Dramatic color and form make 'Lovely Rose' outstanding. Upright petals exude elegance through their color, texture, and posture. The two rows of luscious pink petals appear darker at the base and lighten slightly at the upper edges. Blooms are held just at the top of the dark green foliage. Very strong stems contribute to this distinctive peony.

KIND Herbaceous hybrid

COLOR Pink

FLORAL FORM Single

FRAGRANCE Not noted

SEASON Early

HEIGHT To 32 inches (81 cm)

SUPPORT Not needed

NOTE 'Lovely Rose' is considered one of the best of Saunders's Lobata hybrids. These hybrids introduced exciting colors to bush peonies.

AWARDS APS Award of Landscape Merit

'Ludovica'

Arthur P. Saunders, 1941
UNITED STATES

Glowing shades of clear, warm, rosy-pink to coral blooms will draw you back again and again. The wonderfully rounded petals form graceful, large-cupped flowers. Even as they mature, they hold their form. This shorter peony for the front of the border saves your garden from visitors stepping on other perennials in their rush to see it.

KIND Herbaceous hybrid

COLOR Pink

FLORAL FORM Semidouble

FRAGRANCE Not significant

SEASON Midseason

HEIGHT 28 inches (71 cm)

SUPPORT Not needed

NOTE This is one of Saunders's legendary Lobata hybrids, renowned for their distinctive pink to salmon and coral tones. 'Ludovica' is considered the warmest soft-pink of the era.

AWARDS APS Gold Medal 1999

'Luxor'

Hans P. Sass, 1933
UNITED STATES

A bloom fit for the Queen of Sheba. Luxuriously petal-filled, double, white blooms waft a mild fragrance. Serves well in the garden as a nicely formed plant. One of Carol's special favorites. Has been favorably compared with 'Monsieur Jules Elie' and blooms at the same time.

KIND Lactiflora

COLOR White

FLORAL FORM Double

FRAGRANCE Fragrant

SEASON Midseason

HEIGHT 32 inches (81 cm)

SUPPORT Not needed

'Madame de Verneville'

Félix Crousse, 1885
FRANCE

An heirloom peony treasured for its pleasant rose scent and stately, double, white flowers. A classic for arrangements. White guard petals open to reveal a blush-white center, which quickly transforms into a crown of white, with a few crimson flecks and a glow of yellow from the inner base. Long regarded as an excellent cut flower. Light-green foliage works well in the border all summer long.

KIND Lactiflora

COLOR White to blush white

FLORAL FORM Double

FRAGRANCE Very fragrant

SEASON Early midseason

HEIGHT 31 inches (79 cm)

SUPPORT May be needed

CUT FLOWER Excellent

NOTE Jeanne de Verneville, the half-sister of Louis XIII, was the historic Madame de Verneville. American playwright Carol M. Rice has written *One Night in the Garden* about this extraordinary woman. In the realm of peonies, Alice Harding recommended 'Madame de Verneville' as a peony of distinction and beauty at low cost, while Dr. Upjohn savored her "maiden blush."

'Maestro'

Edward Auten, 1957
UNITED STATES

'Maestro' definitely puts on a command performance. Dark-red flowers with yellow stamens interspersed among the petals and at the center are a joyful expression of nature. Sturdy stems hold blooms erect in the garden and bouquets, all the better for appreciating the light fragrance. The color is very hard to capture with a camera; it's one of the darkest reds.

KIND Lactiflora
COLOR Dark red
FLORAL FORM Double
FRAGRANCE Lightly fragrant
SEASON Midseason
HEIGHT 33 inches (84 cm)
SUPPORT Not needed

'Mahogany'

Lyman D. Glasscock, 1937
UNITED STATES

The deep-mahogany bloom is anchored by illuminating lighter flares, deep in the petals, surrounding light yellow staminodes. A prizewinner for many characteristics: intensity of flower color, simplicity of form, and foliage cleanliness.

KIND Herbaceous hybrid
COLOR Red
FLORAL FORM Japanese
FRAGRANCE Not noted
SEASON Early
HEIGHT To 36 inches (91 cm)
SUPPORT Not needed
NOTE Sometimes listed as a single form: the condition of the stamens versus the staminodes determines the Japanese form.

AWARDS APS Award of Landscape Merit; APS Gold Medal 2015

'Many Happy Returns'

Donald Hollingsworth, 1986
UNITED STATES

Stunning in the garden, rapturous in a bouquet, 'Many Happy Returns' will garner you compliments from your guests, and some of those compliments may be tinged with jealousy. The red tones are warm and sometimes highlighted by slightly yellow-tinted petals. The form shows the Japanese ancestry, but with a dynamic petal-ball in the center that grows into a bomb-type double. Absolutely fabulous in arrangements.

KIND Herbaceous hybrid

COLOR Red

FLORAL FORM Japanese to bomb-type double

FRAGRANCE None

SEASON Midseason

HEIGHT 34 inches (86 cm)

SUPPORT Not needed

CUT FLOWER Excellent

NOTE 'Many Happy Returns' flaunts the best of three peonies in its complex parentage: warm red tones, the visually delightful (if difficult to classify) floral form, and overall vigor. We wish for more like this medium-size flower that is nice for floral design.

AWARDS APS Award of Landscape Merit; APS Gold Medal 2007

'May Lilac'

Arthur P. Saunders, 1950
UNITED STATES

Delightful, cup-shaped, fragrant blooms that stay lilac-colored in cool climates. The distinctive color makes mature plants showstoppers in the garden. 'May Lilac' shows the large, light-green, rounded foliage of its *P. macrophylla* parent, making it a nice landscape contrast to the Lactiflora peonies. The stems typically bear no side buds, making them ideal for bouquets where one flower per stem is desirable.

KIND Herbaceous hybrid
COLOR Lilac
FLORAL FORM Semidouble
FRAGRANCE Very fragrant
SEASON Early
HEIGHT 32 inches (81 cm)
SUPPORT Not needed
CUT FLOWER Fine

'Merry Mayshine'

Arthur P. Saunders / Donald Smetana, 1994
UNITED STATES

A perky, red single, held in nice upright posture. The yellow center is a nice contrast to the bright petals, creating an exceptional harmony to the entire plant. After bloom, the finely cut, dark-green foliage continues to create a nice specimen of a foliage plant and something of a contrast among other garden plants.

KIND Herbaceous hybrid
COLOR Red
FLORAL FORM Single
FRAGRANCE Fragrant
SEASON Early
HEIGHT To 30 inches (76 cm)
SUPPORT Not needed
NOTE The cut-leaf foliage shows the parentage of the fern-leaf peony, *P. tenuifolia*.

AWARDS APS Award of Landscape Merit

'Minnie Shaylor'

Egbert J. Shaylor, 1919
UNITED STATES

Dressed for the ball, 'Minnie Shaylor' turns out in a fluffy white gown, accented by clear yellow and anchored by a touch of red. The several rows of crepelike, ruffled petals are firmly held close to the foliage by stout stems. Side buds extend the bloom period, as they bloom later than the central flower. A classic bloom to be much enjoyed. Often used by home gardeners for bouquets.

KIND Lactiflora

COLOR White

FLORAL FORM Semidouble

FRAGRANCE None

SEASON Midseason

HEIGHT 33 inches (84 cm)

SUPPORT Not needed

CUT FLOWER Wonderful

NOTE One of 37 peonies introduced by Egbert Shaylor, of Auburndale, Massachusetts, of which at least 10 were named for Shaylor women.

AWARDS APS Award of Landscape Merit; APS Best in Show 1986

'Miss America'

James R. Mann / Julius van Steen, 1936
UNITED STATES

Beautiful, fresh, fragrant, pert, and pure white, 'Miss America' is certainly one of the peony ideals of mid-twentieth century aesthetics. This selection has been winning gardeners' hearts and show trophies since shortly after it was introduced and still ranks well eighty years later. Large, cupped, white petals are centered with light yellow stamens and white carpel tips, which all combine to give the flower a pert appearance.

KIND Lactiflora
COLOR White; buds initially blush pink
FLORAL FORM Semidouble
FRAGRANCE Fragrant
SEASON Midseason
HEIGHT To 36 inches (91 cm)
SUPPORT Not needed
NOTE Mann and van Steen likely felt this peony celebrated the resolute and hopeful dreams of the times. Named after the Miss America Pageant in Atlantic City, New Jersey, it famously celebrated some of the changing roles of women; a key ideal was vigor. 'Miss America' has also been used in breeding other peonies.

AWARDS APS Gold Medal 1956; APS Best in Show 1980; RHS Award of Garden Merit 2012

'Mister Ed'

Klehm Nursery, 1980
UNITED STATES

The only peony with two colors of flowers on the same bush make it the perfect subject for the small garden. 'Mr. Ed' is loved for the fragrant flowers that, on the same bush or even the same flower, can be luscious blush pink or pink, or wonderfully in between. Vigorous. Widely used as a cut flower.

KIND Lactiflora

COLOR Blush to pink

FLORAL FORM Bomb-type double

FRAGRANCE Fragrant

SEASON Midseason

HEIGHT To 36 inches (91 cm)

SUPPORT Needed

CUT FLOWER Excellent

NOTE 'Mr. Ed' was developed from 'Monsieur Jules Elie'. Consider growing both.

'Monsieur Jules Elie'

Félix Crousse, 1888
FRANCE

A huge ball of lively rose pink with curlicue petals, this is a classic French peony. Fragrance greets you as the bloom leans toward you, inviting you to echo its leaning. Who can resist the temptation to come closer for a waft of floral perfume? The fragrance is sometimes compared with roses; perhaps such roses should be compared with peonies. The bomb flower form easily opens when cut in bud, as the guard petals readily release the smaller center petals. In the garden, the stems do best with some support, especially in rainy conditions. Widely used as a cut flower.

KIND Lactiflora

COLOR Pink

FLORAL FORM Bomb-type double

FRAGRANCE Moderately fragrant

SEASON Midseason

HEIGHT To 36 inches (91 cm)

SUPPORT Needed

CUT FLOWER Fine

NOTE When you need a classic pink peony that has a heavenly perfume, lush, even extravagant petals, and yet is completely sophisticated, 'Monsieur Jules Elie' comes right to mind. The unambiguous fragrance, the handsome pink bomb, and its utter dependability are hard to beat. Alice Harding appreciated the "very large petals which are more intense pink at the base." Dr. Upjohn expressed it crisply: "Should be in every collection." In addition, 'Monsieur Jules Elie' has been essential in many breeder's programs, passing on these traits for well over a century. In Japan, it is sometimes offered as 'Fuji'.

AWARDS RHS Award of Garden Merit 1993

'Moonstone'

Arthur L. Murawska, 1943
UNITED STATES

A delicate, opalescent glow is the essence of this aptly named peony. It begins blush pink, with the center turning a glowing lightest pink, then gradually turning white as the flower matures. A nicely upright plant habit. 'Moonstone's opalescence makes it especially dramatic when backlit or in indirect light.

KIND Lactiflora
COLOR Blush
FLORAL FORM Double
FRAGRANCE Very fragrant
SEASON Midseason
HEIGHT To 36 inches (91 cm)
SUPPORT Not needed

AWARDS APS Gold Medal 1959; APS Best in Show 1999

'Mother's Choice'

Lyman D. Glasscock, 1950
UNITED STATES

Of course, it was mother's choice of peonies! Fluffy, white, large blooms are packed with beautifully arranged petals that add to the flower depth. A few red flecks on the inner petal edges might be present. Pleasing fragrance adds to the allure. In cool, cloudy weather it may bloom blush and turn to white as it opens. This is a sleeper among mid-twentieth century peonies. Truly classic and likely to become a cherished heirloom.

KIND Lactiflora
COLOR White
FLORAL FORM Double
FRAGRANCE Fragrant
SEASON Late midseason
HEIGHT To 34 inches (86 cm)
SUPPORT Needed

AWARDS APS Gold Medal 1993

'Mrs. Franklin D. Roosevelt'

Alonzo B. Franklin, 1932
UNITED STATES

With an elegant, perfectly symmetrical bloom of soft shell pink, this peony is rightly named after an extraordinarily poised lady. The petals continue to form a cup around the center, even as they spread apart. Billowy flowers slightly lighten in color with maturity, eventually becoming a pale pink. Delightful in all stages and definitely a front-of-the-border selection for both its height and elegance. Refined noses describe the fragrance as exquisite.

KIND Lactiflora

COLOR Light pink

FLORAL FORM Double

FRAGRANCE Lightly fragrant

SEASON Midseason

HEIGHT To 28 inches (71 cm)

SUPPORT May be needed

CUT FLOWER Good

NOTE Popular from its introduction and recognized as a classic American selection from the first part of the twentieth century. The breeder's name, Franklin, is pure coincidence for the First Lady's married name. This selection is featured in the Famous Ladies' self-guided tour of the Peony Garden at the University of Michigan's Nichols Arboretum, where it evokes divergent responses. Those who lived through the Great Depression are not likely to ask "Who *was* she?"

AWARDS APS Gold Medal 1948; APS Best in Show 1963, 1984

'My Love'

Donald Hollingsworth, 1992
UNITED STATES

Pearls for affection. The flowers open pearlescent white and bejewel the vigorous plants and your garden. The double flowers mature to white, giving the whole plant a range of tones during its peak season. Strong bushes stand up well to the weather and last all season.

KIND Herbaceous hybrid
COLOR Pearl white, maturing to all white
FLORAL FORM Double
FRAGRANCE Fragrant
SEASON Midseason
HEIGHT 34 inches (86 cm)
SUPPORT Not needed

'Myra MacRae'

Robert Tischler, 1967
UNITED STATES

The unusual lavender-pink color lifts this selection to a noted place among the pinks of peonies. The double flowers are quite large, sometimes 8–9 inches (20–23 cm) across, and are carried well above the foliage. Since 'Myra McRae' blooms relatively late in the season, the color is all the more distinctive and welcome. This exceptionally vigorous plant holds a large flower that will need support against weather in the landscape.

KIND Lactiflora
COLOR Pink
FLORAL FORM Double
FRAGRANCE None
SEASON Late
HEIGHT 30 inches (76 cm).
SUPPORT May be needed
NOTE Named in honor of Tischler's sister.

AWARDS APS Gold Medal 1998

'Nick Shaylor'

Francis H. Allison, 1931
UNITED STATES

The near-perfect peony for flower shape, petal arrangement, strong stems, and good foliage. Call it a 9+, only because it lacks fragrance. One of its virtues is that the petal-packed buds open quite reliably to release the large and stunning flower. Flower color depends upon the weather as it opens: sunny weather produces white flowers; cloudy weather produces pink to blush. The full rose-flower form continues to be outstanding in the garden, in competition, and in bouquets.

KIND Lactiflora

COLOR Blush pink

FLORAL FORM Double

FRAGRANCE None

SEASON Late midseason

HEIGHT To 36 inches (91 cm)

SUPPORT Not needed

NOTE Few peonies continue to garner awards after more than forty years on the market. That 'Nick Shaylor' has done so is a sign that it is a proven and distinguished peony. Even after eighty-five years, 'Nick Shaylor' remains very much in demand.

AWARDS APS Gold Medal 1941, 1972; APS Best in Show 1969

'Nippon Beauty'

Edward Auten, 1927
UNITED STATES

A golden center is framed by deep garnet cupped petals. The unusual peony, now nearly a century in the trade and gardens, is still outstanding. At its introduction, it was awarded a Prize of Special Merit that was nearly $1400 at today's value.

KIND Lactiflora

COLOR Garnet red

FLORAL FORM Japanese

FRAGRANCE Lightly fragrant

SEASON Late

HEIGHT 32 inches (81 cm)

SUPPORT Not needed

NOTE The reddish colored seedpods are delightful in summer floral arrangements.

'Norma Volz'

Albert L. Volz, 1962
UNITED STATES

Sumptuously large, blush flowers open to waft a lovely fragrance. As the flowers mature, they fade to ivory white. Some petals may have crimson flecks, especially toward the edges. Strong stems hold the massive flowers well.

KIND Lactiflora

COLOR Blush pink, maturing to ivory white

FLORAL FORM Double

FRAGRANCE Not noted

SEASON Midseason

HEIGHT 34 inches (86 cm)

SUPPORT May be needed

NOTE Winner of the Myron D. Bigger Plaque the year it was introduced. One of its parents is 'Miss America,' another champion peony.

AWARDS APS Gold Medal 1987

'Nosegay'

Arthur P. Saunders, 1951
UNITED STATES

Delicate-looking, shell- to salmon-pink, single blooms are highlighted by deeper pink carpels, ringed with yellow stamens. If there are elves in the garden, they must dwell here. Pleasantly cut foliage makes for an attractive, verdant bush in the summer garden.

KIND Herbaceous hybrid

COLOR Pink

FLORAL FORM Single

FRAGRANCE None

SEASON Early

HEIGHT 30 inches (76 cm)

SUPPORT Not needed

NOTE A nosegay is a very small floral arrangement that could be worn, similar to a boutonniere. The distinctive colors and foliage are the result of Saunders's experiments crossing *P. mlokosewitschii* and *P. tenuifolia*.

'Old Faithful'

Lyman D. Glasscock / Elizabeth Falk, 1964
UNITED STATES

\Velvety, dark-red, regal, double blooms to mesmerize you and keep you in the garden, contemplating the beauty. The hybrid plant vigor is evident on this variety, in the heavy petal substance, strong stems, plant height, and healthy, dark-green foliage. Blooms are held 6–12 inches (15–30 cm) above the foliage, with one bloom per stem. It is a reference point in the intensely-red hybrid peonies developed during the mid-twentieth century, and much appreciated today.

KIND Herbaceous hybrid
COLOR Dark velvet-red
FLORAL FORM Double
FRAGRANCE Lightly fragrant
SEASON Midseason
HEIGHT 36–40 inches (91–102 cm)
SUPPORT Not needed
CUT FLOWER Excellent
NOTE 'Old Faithful' is Carol's favorite midseason red. Carol knew Elizabeth Falk, daughter of Lyman Glasscock, and the old faithful peony was growing by a building on their property, pretty much ignored. It grew year after year and was finally noticed by Elizabeth. Since nothing had been done with it, she decided it was good enough to register. Thus, the name. The variant spelling is 'Ole Faithful'.

AWARDS APS Award of Landscape Merit; APS Gold Medal 1997

'Pastelegance'

William Seidl, 1989
UNITED STATES

Romance itself. Dreamy, pastel, double blooms, sump-tuously petal-packed, mature to an elegant cream tone throughout. It's enough to make any garden visitor swoon. Strong stems hold the flowers erect, and as a bonus, it's a good landscape peony, too.

KIND Herbaceous hybrid

COLOR Creamy pastel pink

FLORAL FORM Double

FRAGRANCE None

SEASON Midseason

HEIGHT 30 inches (76 cm)

SUPPORT Not needed

NOTE The name says it all. This selection is destined to be a classic of our era. It magically combines the best of its equally distinctive parents, 'Salmon Dream' and 'Lemon Chiffon'.

AWARDS APS Best in Show 2016

'Paul M. Wild'

Gilbert H. Wild & Son, 1964
UNITED STATES

Cheerful, ruby-red blooms resist fading as they mature.
Large and beautifully formed, the flowers are held on
an upright bush, but in harsh weather they may require
support. Light fragrance is an added bonus. Side buds
can be removed at pea size to make the main flower
larger, or leave them on for a longer bloom.

KIND Lactiflora

COLOR Ruby red

FLORAL FORM Double

FRAGRANCE Lightly fragrant

SEASON Late midseason

HEIGHT 36 inches (91 cm)

SUPPORT Needed

CUT FLOWER Excellent

NOTE 'Paul M. Wild' is consistently among the best rated reds,
both for garden enjoyment and use in floral arrangements.

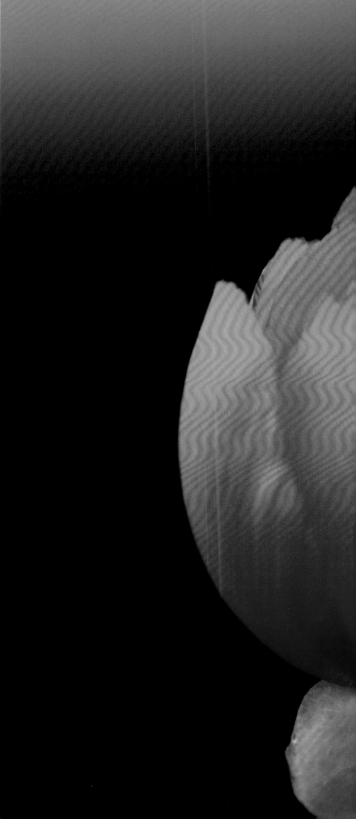

Paeonia peregrina

Philip Miller, 1768
BRITAIN

Beautiful in its simplicity with unusually bright-red flowers that carry an orange tone. Since it's a species, the floral color varies depending on the region of origin. It is the source of blended orange, red, coral, and cherry tones in many cultivars. 'Otto Froebel' (sometimes offered as 'Sunshine') is a well-known selection.

KIND Herbaceous species
COLOR Red
FLORAL FORM Single
FRAGRANCE Not noted
SEASON Early
HEIGHT 32 inches (81 cm)

SUPPORT Not needed
NOTE This wild species is native from southeastern Europe into Turkey. It was named by Philip Miller, who served as the chief gardener at the Chelsea Physic Garden.

'Picotee'

Arthur P. Saunders, 1949
UNITED STATES

Look for floral pixies! Long, rounded, milk-white petals are edged deep magenta-pink, thus, the name. These charmingly dwarf plants with rounded foliage and distinctive crimson stems are ideal for rock gardens and the front of garden borders.

KIND Herbaceous hybrid

COLOR White

FLORAL FORM Single

FRAGRANCE Lightly fragrant

SEASON Very early

HEIGHT 18 inches (46 cm)

SUPPORT Not needed

'Pietertje Vriend Wagenaar'

Nicholas J. Friend, 1996
UNITED STATES

Mother Nature enhanced this pink bloom with darker "paint flecks." This hybrid is thought to be a chance seedling (thank you, bees!) between two well-loved peonies that were being grown together—'Kansas' and 'Sarah Bernhardt'. It has the best of both parents.

KIND Lactiflora

COLOR Dark pink

FLORAL FORM Double

FRAGRANCE Not noted

SEASON Midseason

HEIGHT 33 inches (83 cm)

SUPPORT Not needed

NOTE It is named for the breeder's mother. One of the few other similarly "flecked" peonies is 'The Fawn' by American B. B. Wright.

'Pink Derby'

Myron D. Bigger, 1966
UNITED STATES

'Pink Derby' perfectly resembles a bowl of confetti. Mixed pink-and-cream petaloids mound inside the bold pink petals. The two-toned flowers show well the bomb-type, named after the frozen dessert, bombe glacé. The solid pink outer petals are the plate on which the mound of ice cream rests. The stems bend gracefully.

KIND Lactiflora

COLOR White

FLORAL FORM Bomb-type double

FRAGRANCE Fragrant

SEASON Midseason

HEIGHT To 34 inches (86 cm)

SUPPORT Needed

NOTE This is one of Bigger's most stunning introductions.

AWARDS APS Best in Show 1988

'Pink Hawaiian Coral'

Roy G. Klehm, 1981
UNITED STATES

This exotic beauty is absolutely luscious in the garden or bouquets. The bright, reddish pink, coral bloom exudes a tropical aura and is the most fragrant of the coral-toned peonies. It has a rose form with slightly larger guard petals enclosing slightly smaller inner petals, accented with lemon-yellow stamens in the center. Color-fading occurs pleasingly with maturity. Third-year plants will reward your patience with the full-size blooms.

KIND Herbaceous hybrid

COLOR Coral, and fading slightly lighter, even to include warm, creamy tones

FLORAL FORM Semidouble

FRAGRANCE Fragrant

SEASON Early

HEIGHT To 34 inches (86 cm)

SUPPORT Usually not needed

CUT FLOWER Excellent

NOTE 'Pink Hawaiian Coral' has been consistently popular with gardeners and as a cut flower, ever since its introduction. The range of color tones, the fragrance, and the strong stems make this an outstanding introduction.

AWARDS APS Award of Landscape Merit; APS Gold Medal 2000

'Pink Pearl'

Hans P. Sass, 1937
UNITED STATES

A pink pearl it is! Very fragrant, nicely formed double pink flowers on strong stems make this desirable for the garden and vase. The relatively short plants should be near the front of the border.

KIND Lactiflora
COLOR Pink
FLORAL FORM Double
FRAGRANCE Very fragrant
SEASON Midseason
HEIGHT 30 inches (76 cm)
SUPPORT Not needed

'President Lincoln'

Archie M. Brand, 1928
UNITED STATES

Bold deep red blooms with a glowing yellow center honor a legendary American. Still one of the darkest red peonies with the bonus of light fragrance.

KIND Lactiflora
COLOR Red
FLORAL FORM Single
FRAGRANCE Lightly fragrant
SEASON Midseason
HEIGHT 36 inches (91 cm)
SUPPORT Not needed
NOTE This is one of the few red peonies with fragrance.

'Princess Margaret'

Arthur L. Murawska, 1960
UNITED STATES

If you enjoyed the British Broadcasting Company's *Downton Abbey*, you'll rave over the sophisticated elegance of 'Princess Margaret'. Statuesque, large, dark pink flowers are endowed with pleasant fragrance. Strong stems hold the flowers well, but many need staking simply because of the size of the flowers.

KIND Lactiflora
COLOR Dark pink
FLORAL FORM Double
FRAGRANCE Fragrant
SEASON Late midseason
HEIGHT 34 inches (86 cm)
SUPPORT Needed
NOTE Another noteworthy selection by Murawska that will likely become a mid-twentieth century classic. Named in honor of the Princess, with the permission of her mother, Queen Elizabeth.

AWARDS APS Best in Show 1978

'Princess Bride'

Roy G. Klehm, 1988
UNITED STATES

Fit for a royal wedding, large guard petals make a distinguished cup around the full mound of smaller central petals. Pure white, double flowers grace this compact plant and are held aloft with strong stems. Enjoy the fragrance in the garden, as well as in arrangements.

KIND Lactiflora
COLOR White
FLORAL FORM Bomb-type double
FRAGRANCE Fragrant
SEASON Early
HEIGHT 30 inches (76 cm)
SUPPORT Not needed

'Raspberry Charm'

Samuel E. Wissing / Roy G. Klehm, 1985
UNITED STATES

Bold and confident. The lovely raspberry-red petals surround a center of golden stamens, forming a stunning color combination. Plants bloom reliably, and flowers are held on strong stems. This one stole Carol's heart at first sight.

KIND Herbaceous hybrid

COLOR Raspberry red

FLORAL FORM Semidouble

FRAGRANCE None

SEASON Midseason

HEIGHT 36 inches (91 cm)

SUPPORT Not needed

NOTE Related to 'Coral Charm', but quite a different color. Enjoy growing and displaying both. Wissing originated only twelve peonies that were registered, but all are sublime.

'Raspberry Sundae'

Carl G. Klehm, 1968
UNITED STATES

Think of a scoop of vanilla ice cream drizzled with raspberry sauce. That's 'Raspberry Sundae'. Carol calls it the cheerleader of the garden. A bright, cheerful pink, underlaid with vanilla yellow and held aloft by a row of large, pale pink guard petals. Each flower is an individual, some with more yellow, some with fewer petals, but all are delightful. The distinctive form and color, enhanced by the mild sweet fragrance, make this a likely classic peony for generations ahead. Stems benefit from support, or the heavy flowers will make each stem flex, some more than others.

KIND Lactiflora

COLOR Pink center, pale cream towards the base, with paler pink guard petals

FLORAL FORM Bomb-type double

FRAGRANCE Quite pleasantly mild

SEASON Midseason

HEIGHT To 36 inches (91 cm)

SUPPORT Needed

CUT FLOWER Excellent

NOTE There simply was nothing quite like 'Raspberry Sundae' among herbaceous peonies before it was introduced, and to great acclaim. Belongs in every garden where color-nuanced artists may appear.

'Red Charm'

Lyman D. Glasscock, 1944
UNITED STATES

A sensational, crimson-red, gigantic flower as tall as it is wide, it metamorphoses from a tight red ball into a gigantic mound of numerous long, narrow petals. Bring blooms into the house so you can revel in all its stages of maturity. The overall impact is why terms as "sensational," "eye-catcher," "top winner," and "incredibly intense" are used in almost all descriptions of it. Then, in its final act, the small petals fall, usually in sections, over a period of days, to make a new mound on the table. Everyone enjoys it, so it is an easy decision to include in your garden. There will be only one bloom per stem, but each is so huge a stem could not hold more. As a shorter peony, it calls for placement in the front of the flower bed. A slight clove fragrance adds to the appeal.

KIND Herbaceous hybrid

COLOR Deep red

FLORAL FORM Bomb-type double

FRAGRANCE Slightly fragrant

SEASON Early

HEIGHT To 32 inches (81 cm)

SUPPORT Usually not needed

CUT FLOWER Excellent

NOTE The bold and deep red color perfectly captures the confident color sense of the mid-twentieth century, yet is fully appropriate in modern gardens, too. This is one of David's all-time favorites, and he can't imagine his garden without it.

AWARDS APS Gold Medal 1956; APS Best in Show 1951, 1965

'Red Grace'

Lyman D. Glasscock / Roy G. Klehm, 1980
UNITED STATES

A stunning ball of red, 'Red Grace' nods on the stem from the weight of the many petals. It has the same deep red color value as 'Red Charm', but presented in the form of a globe when mature. You think the flower is open, but wait, it is still opening, and opening. This is one of those flowers that keeps you in the garden waiting for its full majesty to be displayed. And yes, there is a slight fragrance as a bonus. Not a flower for the timid.

KIND Herbaceous hybrid
COLOR Deep red
FLORAL FORM Bomb-type double
FRAGRANCE Lightly fragrant
SEASON Midseason
HEIGHT 32 inches (81 cm)
SUPPORT Needed

NOTE Although Glasscock bred both 'Red Charm' and 'Red Grace', they were evidently developed years apart, and the parentage of this beauty is not clear. Thankfully, Klehm recognized this for the stunning peony it is and introduced it to horticulture. The rest is history.

'Red Red Rose'

Arthur P. Saunders, 1942
UNITED STATES

Thrilling, vivid red makes the heart jump. The blood-red flowers with ruffled petals almost shine from the intense color and always get attention. When the flowers open, the golden stamens in the middle punch the red color. A mysteriously light fragrance emanates from the flower-covered plants. Strong stems hold the flowers above the foliage.

KIND Herbaceous hybrid
COLOR Red
FLORAL FORM Semidouble
FRAGRANCE Slightly fragrant
SEASON Midseason
HEIGHT 32 inches (81 cm)
SUPPORT Not needed
NOTE This is one of Saunders's notable red Lobata hybrids. The intense color deserves the double red in the name. It you like colors hot, you'll have to have 'Red Red Rose'.

'Rhapsody'

Edward Auten, 1956
UNITED STATES

Pink petals encircle a mound of glowing ivory mini-petals. Flowers frequently accented by a puff of pink and red markings in the center. Exquisite.

KIND Lactiflora
COLOR Pink and ivory yellow
FLORAL FORM Japanese
FRAGRANCE Very fragrant
SEASON Midseason
HEIGHT 30 inches (76 cm)
SUPPORT Not needed
NOTE In a letter from Auten, noted as "very odd and distinct." We'd say delightfully different and distinct.

'Rose Heart'

William Bockstoce / Henry Landis, 1974
UNITED STATES

This is one your neighbors won't believe. Flowers open deep pink throughout. Then, the outer petals fade to a soft pink, while the tightly packed inner petals retain the deep pink color. The effect is very unusual and quite fetching. Ideal for blending floral pinks in the garden and bouquets.

KIND Lactiflora
COLOR Deep pink
FLORAL FORM Double
FRAGRANCE Lightly fragrant
SEASON Early
HEIGHT 33 inches (84 cm)
SUPPORT May be needed
CUT FLOWER Excellent, but when cut in bud, color will remain pink
NOTE Bred before 1955, but not introduced under this name until 1974. Some things in life are worth the wait, and this was one.

'Roselette'

Arthur P. Saunders, 1950
UNITED STATES

Spring arrives with stunning simplicity in this blush-pink, single, very early bloomer. The glowing flowers are held like chalices high above the foliage, just beckoning garden pixies with a tempting note of light spring fragrance. The textured petals and a cluster of yellow anthers add to the visual delight. In a word, sweet. The early color is a delight in the garden and helps announce peony season is finally here.

KIND Herbaceous hybrid
COLOR Blush pink
FLORAL FORM Single
FRAGRANCE Lightly fragrant
SEASON Very early
HEIGHT 34 inches (86 cm)
SUPPORT Not needed

AWARDS APS Award of Landscape Merit

'Salmon Dream'

David L. Reath, 1979
UNITED STATES

Prim, proper, and perfect describes 'Salmon Dream'. It makes Carol think of Queen Elizabeth or Princess Diana, for its elegance in holding its petals cupped in such precision, for its purity of color, and for its lack of pretense. It is refined simplicity at the highest level. Nice bush form with sufficient foliage to accent the bloom.

KIND Herbaceous hybrid
COLOR Pink
FLORAL FORM Semidouble
FRAGRANCE None
SEASON Midseason
HEIGHT To 33 inches (84 cm)
SUPPORT Not needed
CUT FLOWER Excellent
NOTE The distinctively warm color implied in the name is not often seen in peonies and makes 'Salmon Dream' so valuable in gardens and bouquets.

AWARDS APS Award of Landscape Merit; APS Gold Medal 2008; APS Best in Show 2015

'Rozella'

David L. Reath, 1990
UNITED STATES

A compact plant that presents its flowers well. As the flower matures, the dark pink petals frost to silver on the edges, providing a pleasing two-toned effect. 'Rozella' is a must-have for the busy gardener or the nongardener. It is a robust plant that flowers profusely, doesn't need staking, and brightens the garden in the late spring.

KIND Herbaceous hybrid
COLOR Pink
FLORAL FORM Double
FRAGRANCE Lightly fragrant
SEASON Late
HEIGHT 31 inches (79 cm)
SUPPORT Not needed

AWARDS APS Award of Landscape Merit

'Sarah Bernhardt'

Émile Lemoine, 1906
FRANCE

A luscious, romantic-pink, fragrant, and full-double peony, 'Sarah Bernhardt' is an heirloom variety that has withstood disease and fashion for over one hundred years and is still going strong. It's widely available and has been used as a cut flower for generations in North America, Europe, and Japan. The soft shell-pink petals surprise you with a few crimson flecks on the center petal-edges. The bud also contains streaks of red, but they are not visible once the flower opens. If you've ever wondered which peony might be Grandma's favorite pink double, you're likely correct with 'Sarah Bernhardt'.

KIND Lactiflora

COLOR Medium pink

FLORAL FORM Double

FRAGRANCE Fragrant, but not strongly so

SEASON Late

HEIGHT To 36 inches (91 cm)

SUPPORT Needed

CUT FLOWER Excellent

NOTE Named for the famous actress. Has been continuously popular whenever soft-pink peonies are considered. Shortly after it was introduced, Alice Harding listed it as "rare and exquisite." Dr. Upjohn praised its "perfect form."

AWARDS RHS Award of Garden Merit 1993

'Scarlet O'Hara'

Lyman D. Glasscock / Elizabeth Falk, 1956
UNITED STATES

A large, fiery-red bloom, reaching for the heavens with its height and held aloft by its magnificent lush foliage. Stunning flowers centered on light red carpel tips surrounded by a multitude of yellow stamens are frequently visited by bees. It's all hypnotizing. The foliage is deeply veined and attractive. A cross of two peony species, this selection demonstrates the resulting hybrid vigor.

KIND Herbaceous hybrid

COLOR Red

FLORAL FORM Single

FRAGRANCE None

SEASON Early

HEIGHT To 36 inches (91 cm)

SUPPORT Not needed

NOTE Anyone who has seen *Gone with the Wind* will recognize why this peony is named 'Scarlet O'Hara'. Everything about it is strong willed, and it is destined to become a classic American peony from the mid-twentieth century, even without the link to one of the greatest American movies.

AWARDS APS Award of Landscape Merit

'Sea Shell'

Hans P. Sass, 1937
UNITED STATES

Bright, satiny, pink flowers held on tall stems above the mint-green foliage combine to exemplify grace and elegance. The large petals make a sea of color in a grouping, and the golden center adds a touch of sunshine to the appearance. The color lightens pleasingly with as the flower matures. An upright and vigorous grower in the garden with flowers held high, this peony is a good candidate for planting a bit further back in the perennial garden.

KIND Lactiflora

COLOR Pink

FLORAL FORM Single

FRAGRANCE Lightly fragrant

SEASON Midseason

HEIGHT To 37 inches

SUPPORT Not needed

CUT FLOWER Fine

NOTE This is one of Sass's noteworthy *P. lactiflora* cultivars. Once more, his abilities and discriminating eye have resulted in an elegant plant with many notes of distinction.

AWARDS APS Gold Medal 1990

'Shawnee Chief'

Myron D. Bigger, 1940
UNITED STATES

Proud and bravura floral performance. A prolific bloomer with double, red, fragrant flowers, a bit after the midpoint of the peony season. The three outer rings of petals are larger than the central ones and have been compared to a chieftain's headdress. The name is clearly an honorific. Good cut flower on strong stems. A desirable color for the gardener who revels in red.

KIND Lactiflora
COLOR Red
FLORAL FORM Double
FRAGRANCE Fragrant
SEASON Late midseason
HEIGHT 36 inches (91 cm)
SUPPORT Not needed
CUT FLOWER Excellent
NOTE The flower color has been reported to be darker in the hotter zones where peonies can be grown. According to Donald Hollingsworth, this was the peony Bigger most recommended for cemetery plantings in post–World War II America. Bigger appreciated its buds, as he felt, of all his peonies, they most resemble a rose.

'Shirley Temple'

Louis Smirnow, before 1948
UNITED STATES

Delicate clouds of blush-white petals fade to white with occasional red edges on the inner petals. Truly a floral dream come true. The large, rose-type, double flowers are lightly fragrant. Bring 'Shirley Temple' indoors in bouquets or by herself, because you won't want to miss a moment.

KIND Lactiflora
COLOR White
FLORAL FORM Double rose-form
FRAGRANCE Lightly fragrant
SEASON Midseason
HEIGHT 34 inches (86 cm)
SUPPORT Usually not needed
CUT FLOWER Excellent
NOTE Named for one of America's movie stars. One of the parents is 'Festiva Maxima', which is itself a superb and classic French peony. The fruit didn't fall far from the tree here.

'Snow Mountain'

Myron D. Bigger, 1946
UNITED STATES

Just as the name promises, flowers mature to a loose, high mountain of snow-white petals. An inner glow of yellow, sometimes accented with red flecks, completes the idyllic scene. An excellent choice when snow-white flowers are needed.

KIND Lactiflora
COLOR White
FLORAL FORM Bomb-type double
FRAGRANCE Lightly fragrant
SEASON Midseason
HEIGHT 34 inches (86 cm)
SUPPORT Not needed
NOTE Similar to 'Monsieur Jules Elie' in floral form, but not color.

'Sparkling Star'

Myron D. Bigger, 1953
UNITED STATES

Joyful, cheerful, bright, dark-pink flowers hold their color well. Strong stems pose these floral stars so you can enjoy their light fragrance, while the side buds provide a prolonged period of bloom. 'Sparkling Star' has earned a reputation for standing up well to rain, a consideration for cut-flower growers, and staking is not necessary, even with the side buds. Good, bright-green foliage endures through the summer.

KIND Lactiflora
COLOR Pink
FLORAL FORM Single
FRAGRANCE Lightly fragrant
SEASON Early
HEIGHT 30 inches (76 cm)
SUPPORT Not needed

AWARDS APS Gold Medal 1995

'Stardust'

Lyman D. Glasscock / Elizabeth Falk, 1964
UNITED STATES

All the glamour of the big screen, stardust itself. Large, wavy, white petals encircle golden stamens and green carpels, making a very attractive and poised composition. Floral fragrance adds to the allure.

KIND Lactiflora
COLOR White
FLORAL FORM Single
FRAGRANCE Fragrant
SEASON Midseason
HEIGHT 34 inches (86 cm)
SUPPORT Not needed
NOTE Thought to be the grandchild of 'Le Cygne', one of the most highly rated, fragrant, white peonies for generations. Truly peony royalty, fit for its own starring roles.

'Sugar n' Spice'

Allan Rogers, 1988
UNITED STATES

Such a color, so early in the peony season. Symmetrical flowers have slightly fluted, salmon-orange to pink petals. A delightful color combination. Foliage performs well in the garden through the season.

KIND Herbaceous hybrid
COLOR Salmon orange to pink
FLORAL FORM Single
FRAGRANCE None
SEASON Very early
HEIGHT 34 inches (86 cm)
SUPPORT Not needed

'Summer Glow'

Donald Hollingsworth, 1992
UNITED STATES

A peachy color in peonies. Completely full flowers add to the allure by maturing to an elegant ivory. An erect plant habit with sturdy stems that hold the blooms well in the garden and in vases. Since the plant is inherently slow to increase in size, this selection is not common in the market, but worth finding and cherishing.

KIND Herbaceous hybrid
COLOR Peachy yellow to yellow
FLORAL FORM Double
FRAGRANCE Not noted
SEASON Midseason
HEIGHT 34 inches (86 cm)
SUPPORT Not needed
NOTE One of Hollingsworth's distinctive introductions, 'Summer Glow' shows his work towards stunning yellow herbaceous hybrid peonies continued even as he developed now-well-known yellow intersectionals as 'Garden Treasure'. There is nothing like it.

'Sword Dance'

Edward Auten, 1933
UNITED STATES

Rich red, single flowers hold an explosion of broad, red-streaked petaloids. They are indeed the festive revelry of a brace of swords dancing with vigor and pride. The strong, red color holds even in bright sunlight. Very floriferous, so the dance keeps on going. There ought to be a modern tartan based on these colors for people who'd like to join in. At Adelman's display garden, an unusual and outstanding flower that drew attention even as a first-year plant.

KIND Lactiflora
COLOR Red
FLORAL FORM Japanese
FRAGRANCE None
SEASON Late
HEIGHT 36 inches (91 cm)
SUPPORT Not needed
NOTE Auten introduced many spectacularly dark, even boldly intense lactiflora peonies in the first half of the twentieth century. Too many now seem to be lost. Fortunately, 'Sword Dance' has always been highly regarded and continues to have admirers today, including both the authors. Given this selection's 2014 Award, many others agree.

AWARDS APS Award of Landscape Merit

'The Mackinac Grand'

David L. Reath, 1992
UNITED STATES

A brilliant, ruffled, orange-red bloom that shows up clear across the garden. The satin sheen glows, surrounding the opulent yellow center that encloses the red carpel tips. The flower is a host to bees, who gather pollen and also disperse it. A vigorous plant that holds one bloom per stem and so requires no additional support.

KIND Herbaceous hybrid
COLOR Red
FLORAL FORM Single
FRAGRANCE None
SEASON Early midseason
HEIGHT To 36 inches (91 cm)
SUPPORT Not needed

NOTE Named after the venerable and renowned luxury resort hotel on Mackinac Island in the Upper Peninsula of Michigan. The story goes that Reath, upon staying at the hotel, bartered the naming right in exchange for the bill. The hotel got a bargain.

AWARDS APS Award of Landscape Merit; APS Gold Medal 2013

'Topeka Garnet'

Myron D. Bigger, 1975
UNITED STATES

Love at first sight. The way the plant holds the bloom as an offering to you is spectacular. Somehow it is a different red than other red peonies, attracting many visitors. The satin glow is contrasted by the glossy, dark green foliage. A good garden variety that is medium height and stands up nicely.

KIND Lactiflora
COLOR Red
FLORAL FORM Single
FRAGRANCE None
SEASON Midseason
HEIGHT To 30 inches (76 cm)
SUPPORT Not needed
NOTE Named by the breeder to honor Topeka, Kansas, where he did his hybridizing.

AWARDS APS Award of Landscape Merit;
APS Gold Medal 2012

'Touch of Class'

Roy G. Klehm, 1999
UNITED STATES

Elegantly simple, and simply elegant. Two rows of pink petals cup around the creamy toned mound of well-packed petaloids. Visually pleasing. Side buds extend the season.

KIND Lactiflora
COLOR Pink and creamy white
FLORAL FORM Anemone, sometimes more complex
FRAGRANCE None
SEASON Midseason
HEIGHT 32 inches (81 cm)
SUPPORT May be needed

'Tropicana'

Jack Nordick, 2012
UNITED STATES

A deep hue of warm dark coral makes this plant a diva that will attract attention from across the garden! A unique and exciting color in peonies. Emerging foliage has a bronze hue that becomes green as the season warms and shows botrytis resistance.

KIND Herbaceous hybrid

COLOR Deep coral

FLORAL FORM Semidouble

FRAGRANCE Not noted

SEASON Midseason

HEIGHT To 42 inches (107 cm)

SUPPORT Not needed

NOTE 'Coral Sunset' is the mother and the bees did the rest! It's not clear which pollen-parent helps account for the remarkable color. Received the Seedling of Distinction award at the APS Exhibition in 2012.

'Walter Mains'

Walter Mains, 1957
UNITED STATES

A timeless beauty that has never been out of fashion. 'Walter Mains' has intensely toned burgundy-red petals that incurve slightly to cup around a visually striking center of staminodes that are each red, gold, and white. A floral fantasia and unlike any other peony. Robust bushes work well in the summer border.

KIND Herbaceous hybrid
COLOR Burgundy-red
FLORAL FORM Japanese
FRAGRANCE None
SEASON Midseason
HEIGHT 33 inches (84 cm)
SUPPORT Not needed
CUT FLOWER Stunning

AWARDS APS Gold Medal 1974

'White Cap'

George E. Winchell, 1956
UNITED STATES

Bold colors will snap everyone to attention. Dark pink- to raspberry-red petals surround the ivory-white petaloids that are slightly infused with the petal colors and that fade to white as the petaloids mature. Absolutely stunning yet pleasing color and textural contrasts. Robust plant in the garden, including after bloom season.

KIND Lactiflora
COLOR Red and white
FLORAL FORM Japanese
FRAGRANCE Slight
SEASON Midseason
HEIGHT 36 inches (91 cm)
SUPPORT Not needed

AWARDS APS Award of Landscape Merit; APS Gold Medal 1991

'White Innocence'

Arthur P. Saunders, 1947
UNITED STATES

Absolutely unique, dramatic, and unmistakable. Pure white, single flowers with greenish centers are carried higher than on most any other bush peony, to 4 feet (1.2 m) and beyond. The display is all the more remarkable for being relatively late in the season (most singles bloom earlier) and with multiple flowers on each swaying stem. 'White Innocence's floral display has been compared to *Anemone* 'Honorine Jobert,' as well as an Empress magnolia, as *Magnolia* 'Royal Star' is sometimes known. Established plants are reported to bear over two hundred flowers a season. Given the extremely tall stems, staking is needed if the flowers are to be cut.

KIND Herbaceous hybrid
COLOR White
FLORAL FORM Single
FRAGRANCE None
SEASON Late midseason
HEIGHT To 4 feet (1.2 m)
SUPPORT Needed

NOTE This is one of Saunders's lesser-known, but absolutely ravishing, cultivars. Much of the distinction comes from its parentage with *P. emodi*.

Intersectional

Peonies

'Bartzella'

Roger F. Anderson, 1986
UNITED STATES

'Bartzella' is one of the few almost totally yellow full-flowered peonies and already a classic that no garden should be without. Red-infused petal markings at the base of the lemon-yellow flowers create a highlight to set off the golden-yellow anthers and white-tipped carpels. On any given plant, the flower form varies from semidouble to double. Flowers are 6–8 inches across and lemony-perfumed. The bush is dark green with vigorous, large, deeply-cut leaves that make it an outstanding foliage plant throughout the summer. Established plants may bloom for nearly a month. Stems of cut flowers need to be re-cut underwater to prevent wilting.

KIND Intersectional
COLOR Yellow to lemon yellow with red flares
FLORAL FORM Semidouble to double
FRAGRANCE Lightly fragrant
SEASON Midseason
HEIGHT To 34 inches (86 cm)
SUPPORT Not needed
CUT FLOWER Wonderful but short-lived

NOTE When this selection was introduced, it became an immediate sensation. With crisp, large, fragrant, yellow flowers on a perennial peony, a veritable 'Holy Grail' of centuries of aspiration had been bred. Not surprisingly 'Bartzella' was one of the first popular Itoh peonies in North America and remains so today. Since it is sterile, producing neither seed nor pollen, it is a forever-unique reference point or, more accurately, a pinnacle. Its grandeur made the world aware of intersectional peonies.

AWARDS APS Award of Landscape Merit; APS Gold Medal 2006; APS Best in Show 2002; RHS Award of Garden Merit 2012

'Callie's Memory'

Roger F. Anderson, 1999
UNITED STATES

Lovely flowers in glowing pastel colors, highlighted by darker, nearly maroon, center flares make this a striking bloom. Petals have a kiss of maroon pink as a picotee edge. Side buds extend the bloom season. Handsome foliage contributes to the garden all summer long.

KIND Intersectional
COLOR Apricot cream
FLORAL FORM Semidouble to double
FRAGRANCE Lightly fragrant
SEASON Midseason
HEIGHT 30 inches (76 cm)
SUPPORT Not needed

'Canary Brilliants'

Roger F. Anderson, 1999
UNITED STATES

Don't leave for long as this one comes into bloom. Flowers open a light or creamy yellow and then the show begins. Some blooms become more brilliant, while others mature to include warm apricot tones in the center. These wonderful color combinations with healthy foliage make 'Canary Brilliants' desirable in the garden all season long.

KIND Intersectional
COLOR Creamy yellow to apricot
FLORAL FORM Semidouble to double
FRAGRANCE Lightly fragrant
SEASON Midseason
HEIGHT 28 inches (71 cm)
SUPPORT Not needed

AWARDS APS Award of Landscape Merit

'First Arrival'

Roger F. Anderson, 1986
UNITED STATES

'Cora Louise'

Roger F. Anderson, 1986
UNITED STATES

Pure white petals are made even more eye-catching by the luscious deep-pink to purple flares in the center of the flower. The semidouble blooms are absolutely stunning, with a light fragrance adding to the allure. The flowers of this reliable garden plant are held well above dark green leaves, which are deeply cut, reflecting the tree peony parent. The bush is sensational when covered in bloom and keeps its pleasing shrub shape throughout the summer.

KIND Intersectional
COLOR White with lavender flares
FLORAL FORM Semidouble to double
FRAGRANCE Lightly fragrant
SEASON Midseason
HEIGHT To 24 inches (60 cm)
SUPPORT Not needed
NOTE 'Cora Louise' honors one of Anderson's grandmothers and is among the earliest Itoh (intersectional) peonies.

Fantastic pinks. 'First Arrival' blooms so abundantly that an established plant is covered in flowers. Part of the excitement, beyond the sheer number of flowers, is the petals' color shift from lavender-pink to paler pinks as the flowers mature. But, amazingly, the red flares on the petals don't fade, making a dramatic show. The lightly fragrant semidouble to double flowers are held close to the foliage and are more lavender in cool climates, pinker in warm climates. The rounded bush has attractive, deeply-cut foliage that stays attractive through the summer. 'First Arrival' is simply gorgeous, lightly fragrant, needs no staking, and is reliable, the best attributes of a bush peony.

KIND Intersectional
COLOR Lavender-pink
FLORAL FORM Semidouble
FRAGRANCE Lightly fragrant
SEASON Midseason
HEIGHT 28 inches (71 cm)
SUPPORT Not needed
NOTE 'First Arrival' got its name because it was the first intersectional cross to bloom for Anderson. It shows the value of intersectional peonies, even when in the traditional color range of bush peonies.

'Garden Treasure'

Donald Hollingsworth, 1984
UNITED STATES

Striking yellow, semidouble 'Garden Treasure' is one of the most important peonies of the late-twentieth century, and it is highly fragrant with wonderful, light citrus notes. It opens yellow-gold, then lightens a bit. The large petals have a touch of red at the base, which lightens as the flower matures. The red is partially covered by the yellow stamens, and centered by pink carpel tips. The flowers are held nicely at the surface of the plant, not much above the foliage, and need no further support. The distinctive cut leaves from its tree peony parent make 'Garden Treasure' a visual delight in the perennial border, even after the blooming season is long over. Its six awards across thirteen years are just one indication of this plant's beauty, versatility, and continued appeal.

KIND Intersectional

COLOR Yellow

FLORAL FORM Semidouble

FRAGRANCE Very fragrant

SEASON Mid to late

HEIGHT To 30 inches (76 cm

SUPPORT Not needed

CUT FLOWER Excellent

NOTE This dazzling, yellow selection is one of the first intersectional peonies to gain great attention. There is absolutely no doubt it will be treasured for generations to come. As to Hollingsworth, who developed it, Thomas Jefferson stated it well: "The greatest service which can be rendered any country is to add a useful plant to its culture."

AWARDS APS Award of Landscape Merit; APS Gold Medal 1996; APS Best in Show 2001, 2004, 2005, 2007

'Gordon E. Simonson'

Roger F. Anderson, 2010
UNITED STATES

Brilliant, fuchsia-pink blooms composed of wavy, pink petals are highlighted by pale, creamy stamens, making a statement of simple beauty. If fuchsia pink is your color, be certain to find a place for this new introduction. Like all intersectional peonies, it has foliage that is useful in the summer garden.

KIND Intersectional
COLOR Fuchsia pink
FLORAL FORM Semidouble
FRAGRANCE None
SEASON Midseason
HEIGHT 26 inches (66 cm)
SUPPORT Not needed

'Hillary'

Roger F. Anderson, 1999
UNITED STATES

You won't want to leave the garden once 'Hillary' begins her spectacle. The huge flowers open red to dark pink and slowly fade to creamy red. The sensational effect comes as the outer petals fade, causing the darker red flares to pop. Spectacular! 'Hillary' becomes a multicolored confection as the older blooms fade and the fresh blooms glow with brilliance. It is a great landscape plant with graceful foliage. The flowers are held close to the foliage.

KIND Intersectional
COLOR Creamy red
FLORAL FORM Semidouble
FRAGRANCE Lightly fragrant
SEASON Midseason
HEIGHT 30 inches (76 cm)
SUPPORT Not needed

NOTE The huge flowers, range of tones, and vigorous growth destine 'Hillary' to be a classic intersectional peony. It was named after Anderson's granddaughter.

AWARDS APS Award of Landscape Merit

'Julia Rose'

Roger F. Anderson, before 2007
UNITED STATES

A veritable confection of color tones on the bush and even in the individual bloom. Each flower opens a cherry red and fades, or matures, to include a range of orange, copper, salmon, yellow and even creamy blends. Established plants may bear over forty blooms in one season. The fine growth habit and foliage make this selection of structural value in the perennial garden long after it has finished blooming.

KIND Intersectional

COLOR Cherry red, maturing to include rose, apricot, copper and yellow-blush tones

FLORAL FORM Single to semidouble

FRAGRANCE Fragrant

SEASON Midseason

HEIGHT 28 inches (71 cm)

SUPPORT Not needed

NOTE 'Julia Rose' is one of the intersectional hybrids that has helped reopen the ideals of beauty in peonies. Among the herbaceous peonies, stable floral colors were long the epitome of perfection. This selection is the herald of an exciting new aesthetic, with its dynamic colors through each bloom's life.

'Kopper Kettle'

Roger F. Anderson, 1999
UNITED STATES

Unusual copper tones of the blooms provide the apt name. The shading is darkest upon opening and matures to include softer yellow tones. The semidouble flowers rest on appealingly dark foliage.

KIND Intersectional

COLOR Orange, red, and yellow tones

FLORAL FORM Semidouble

FRAGRANCE Slightly fragrant

SEASON Midseason

HEIGHT 32 inches (81 cm)

SUPPORT Not needed

NOTE The original spelling used by the breeder is retained here, but the selection was registered and is commonly listed as 'Copper Kettle'. Another step toward an orange peony.

'Lemon Dream'

Roger F. Anderson, 1999
UNITED STATES

Delightful, light-yellow, semidouble blooms pack a surprise and make a statement. From time to time, individual flowers will have sensational lavender streaks or even completely lavender petals. Each flower is different. Occasionally, a half light-yellow, half light-lavender bloom appears. 'Lemon Dream' is a showstopper, even without the bonus of a color extravaganza. The lovely, deeply-cut, glossy, dark-green foliage of its tree peony parent adds to the summer border.

KIND Intersectional

COLOR Yellow, sometimes with lavender streaks and petals

FLORAL FORM Semidouble

FRAGRANCE Slightly fragrant

SEASON Midseason

HEIGHT 34 inches (86 cm)

SUPPORT Not needed

'Love Affair'

Donald Hollingsworth, 2005
UNITED STATES

Stunningly elegant, semidouble, white blooms are presented as symmetrical bowls, usually one per stem. This was the first and best (and still one of the few) white intersectional peonies. The bush provides good foliage for the garden throughout the summer.

KIND Intersectional

COLOR White

FLORAL FORM Semidouble

FRAGRANCE Mild and sweet

SEASON Midseason

HEIGHT 30 inches (76 cm)

SUPPORT Not needed

NOTE This is the white-flowered form of 'Prairie Sunshine', a genetic mutation. If you need both colors in similar floral forms, plant the pair.

'Morning Lilac'

Roger F. Anderson, 1999
UNITED STATES

Hello, Springtime! Lilac to fuchsia-purple blooms can be seen across the garden, or even a field, and beckon everyone in sight, so expect your neighbors and passers-by to drop in. Up close, the flowers range from semidouble to double, and some have subtle striping that can be white to dark fuchsia. The light fragrance is a delightful bonus. Plants have a good garden habit and work well for their summer foliage. 'Morning Lilac' is destined to be a classic among distinctively colored intersectional peonies.

KIND Intersectional

COLOR Fuchsia-purple

FLORAL FORM Semidouble to double

FRAGRANCE Lightly fragrant

SEASON Early

HEIGHT 28 inches (71 cm)

SUPPORT Not needed

'New Millennium'

Roger F. Anderson, 2012
UNITED STATES

Luscious new color in an elegant bloom. Coral pinks vary within and across each petal, attracting attention the moment the flower opens. Light fragrance adds value in the garden and bouquets. Striking foliage makes this an excellent landscape plant. It is one of the exciting new intersectionals becoming available.

KIND Intersectional
COLOR Coral pink
FLORAL FORM Semidouble
FRAGRANCE Lightly fragrant
SEASON Midseason
HEIGHT 28 inches (71 cm)
SUPPORT Not needed
CUT FLOWER Good
NOTE Take your chair to the garden for an hour as this flower will spellbind you as it has us.

'Pastel Splendor'

Roger F. Anderson / William Seidl, 1996
UNITED STATES

Striking maroon flares surround an artistic grouping of creamy carpels that curl in a mass. Many pleasing color tones from pinks to yellows on plants of relatively short stature. Splendid indeed!

KIND Intersectional
COLOR Creamy white with red flares
FLORAL FORM Semidouble
FRAGRANCE Not significant
SEASON Midseason
HEIGHT 33 inches (84 cm)
SUPPORT Not needed

'Scarlet Heaven'

Roger F. Anderson, 1999
UNITED STATES

Stunningly handsome and rightfully popular, 'Scarlet Heaven' has bright red, lightly fragrant, single flowers that boldly declare "Red! right to the tips of the carpels. Think of this as your shining knight, enrobed in a scarlet mantle. Side buds that bloom after the main bloom prolong the enjoyment. The lovely dark-green leaves of the tree peony parent work well in the garden throughout the summer. The flowers are usually held above the foliage. If you're including red tones in your garden or bouquets, 'Scarlet Heaven' is a robust work-horse for you.

KIND Intersectional	**HEIGHT** 28 inches (71 cm)
COLOR Red	**SUPPORT** Not needed
FLORAL FORM Single	**CUT FLOWER** Good
FRAGRANCE Lightly fragrant	
SEASON Midseason	

'Singing in the Rain'

Donald R. Smith, 2002
UNITED STATES

The show goes on! Many color shades are enjoyed during an extended bloom season, ranging from yellow through pink and even into apricot tones. The flowers tend to form groups of three, which are all held near the surface of the foliage.

KIND Intersectional
COLOR Pink to yellow tones
FLORAL FORM Semidouble
FRAGRANCE Lightly fragrant
SEASON Midseason
HEIGHT 36–40 inches (91–102 cm)

SUPPORT Not needed
NOTE This selection was named after a stormy season in which the flowers held up well. It typically has groupings of three blooms like a small bouquet.

'Sonoma Halo'

Irene Tolomeo, 2007
UNITED STATES

Absolutely sensational. 'Sonoma Halo' is drop dead gorgeous and can make you fall in love at first sight. Huge, double, yellow flowers are petal-packed, yet sometimes reveal a touch of red in the center. Vigorous plants support improbably large flowers. This relatively new introduction expands many concepts of what it is to be a peony.

KIND Intersectional
COLOR Yellow
FLORAL FORM Double
FRAGRANCE Fragrant
SEASON Late
HEIGHT 40 inches (102 cm)
SUPPORT Not needed
NOTE A first-year plant exhibited at an APS show won Court of Honor, showing the glamour of this relatively new introduction.

'Sonoma Amethyst'

Irene Tolomeo, 2001
UNITED STATES

Gloriously abundant lavender flowers adorn the entire bush. The lavender color tones are unequaled among peonies. Medium-sized plants are vigorous with attractive foliage that lasts all season and with sidebuds for a prolonged season.

KIND Intersectional
COLOR Lavender
FLORAL FORM Semidouble
FRAGRANCE None
SEASON Midseason
HEIGHT 34 inches (86 cm)
SUPPORT Not needed

'Sonoma Rosy Future'

Irene Tolomeo, 2005
UNITED STATES

A harbinger of wonderful days ahead, 'Sonoma Rosy Future' is a vigorous, almost enthusiastic, bright pink, with darker central flares that show off the yellow stamens and yellow carpel tips. The color matures to a strong and pleasant pink. Has side buds and lovely foliage.

KIND Intersectional
COLOR Brilliant pink
FLORAL FORM Single
FRAGRANCE Not noted
SEASON Midseason
HEIGHT 39 inches (99 cm)
SUPPORT Not needed

'Sonoma Welcome'

Irene Tolomeo, 1999
UNITED STATES

Who wouldn't feel welcome in the garden with this peony in bloom, beckoning? Flowers open apricot colored and fade to a lively, strong yellow. The plant blooms generously. Vigorous bushes work well in the landscape, with attractive leaves that serve all summer long.

KIND Intersectional
COLOR Apricot to warm yellows
FLORAL FORM Single
FRAGRANCE None
SEASON Midseason
HEIGHT 33 inches (84 cm)
SUPPORT Not needed

'Strawberry Blush'

Roger F. Anderson, 2015
UNITED STATES

A spring feast for the eyes. Blooms range from red to red-and-white striped to a solid strawberry color. All have curly yellow stamens centered on strawberry-toned carpel tips. Every flower is an individual marvel.

KIND Intersectional

COLOR Red, sometimes with white stripes

FLORAL FORM Single

FRAGRANCE None

SEASON Midseason

HEIGHT 32 inches (81 cm)

SUPPORT Not needed

NOTE Contemporary intersectional peonies are invigoratingly exciting. Anderson has excelled again.

'Unique'

Roger F. Anderson, 1999
UNITED STATES

Unique, as in distinguished. Single red blooms with reddish-tipped stigmas confidently announce "Red!" in your garden. Stems bear side buds. Has an excellent plant habit, with dark-green foliage that is much more finely cut than other intersectionals.

KIND Intersectional	**SEASON** Midseason
COLOR Red	**HEIGHT** 34 inches (86 cm)
FLORAL FORM Single	**SUPPORT** Not needed
FRAGRANCE Fragrant	

'Watermelon Wine'

Roger F. Anderson, 1999
UNITED STATES

Outstanding new color for the intersectional peonies. Cupped flowers open watermelon red and soon spread to reveal a darker red near the petal bases. As the flowers mature, the petals develop subtly darker and fainter lines that enhance the overall color values. Sensational. The terminal flower is surrounded by three side buds for a long bloom season. Striking cut foliage works well in the summer garden.

KIND Intersectional

COLOR Watermelon red

FLORAL FORM Semidouble

FRAGRANCE None

SEASON Midseason

HEIGHT 34 inches (86 cm)

SUPPORT Not needed

Tree

Peonies

'Age of Gold'

Arthur P. Saunders, 1948
UNITED STATES

Golden ruffled camellias, only writ large. Creamy golden-yellow petals have a red flare at the base, giving the blooms a floral intensity unlike any other. Flowers are held above the foliage. Shrubs typically retain their leaves nearly to the ground all season long. A fast-growing bush.

KIND Lutea hybrid

COLOR Creamy gold

FLORAL FORM Semidouble

FRAGRANCE Fragrant

SEASON Mid tree peony season

HEIGHT 4 feet (1.2 m), may grow taller

SUPPORT Not needed

NOTE One of Saunders's classic tree peony hybrids.

AWARDS APS Gold Medal 1973

'Alice Harding'

Lemoine Nursery, 1935
FRANCE

Bright lemon-yellow flowers—sunshine itself. Petal-packed blooms hang down, so 'Alice Harding' is best planted on a mound or raised area, where she can be viewed from below. Because they nod rather than stand face-up, the flowers are not used in bouquets but to float in a bowl.

KIND Lutea hybrid

COLOR Yellow

FLORAL FORM Semidouble to double

FRAGRANCE Fragrant

SEASON Mid tree peony season

HEIGHT 30 inches (76 cm)

SUPPORT Not needed

NOTE This is the source of yellow in many intersectional hybrids

'Angel Choir'

Roger F. Anderson, 1999
UNITED STATES

Abundant, large, white, semidouble blooms intensified by purple flares truly befit a heavenly choir. Once you've seen 'Angel Choir', you will think you've gone to heaven. A hardy and tall plant.

KIND Suffruticosa group–rockii hybrid
COLOR White with purple flares
FLORAL FORM Semidouble
FRAGRANCE None
SEASON Mid tree peony season
HEIGHT 4 feet (1.2 m)
SUPPORT Not needed

'Angel Emily'

William Seidl / Nathan Bremmer, 2013
UNITED STATES

An extravaganza of lavender-purple bloom means this plant can be the reigning diva of your garden. Semidouble blooms are 6–8 inches (15–20 cm) across. The plant is cold hardy and long-lived with ornamental foliage.

KIND Suffruticosa group–rockii hybrid
COLOR Lavender with darker flares
FLORAL FORM Semidouble
FRAGRANCE None
SEASON Mid tree peony season
HEIGHT To 5 feet (1.5 m)
SUPPORT Not needed
NOTE The introducer had a nine-year old plant with 45 flowers. Sensational!

'Anna Marie'

William Seidl, 1984
UNITED STATES

Lavender-pink flowers with deep raspberry flares are a feast for the eyes. An elegant flower on a vigorous, easily grown plant.

KIND Lutea hybrid
COLOR Lavender-pink
FLORAL FORM Single
FRAGRANCE None
SEASON Mid tree peony season
HEIGHT 48 inches (123 cm)
SUPPORT Not needed
NOTE A fine living tribute to Mr. Seidl's mother.

'Autumn Harvest'

William Seidl, 1989
UNITED STATES

Many outward-facing blooms greet you even from a distance. The very doubled, yellow flowers are flecked with red. This fast-growing plant with deep blue-green foliage works well in the garden.

KIND Lutea hybrid
COLOR Straw yellow with red flecking
FLORAL FORM Double
FRAGRANCE Not noted
SEASON Mid tree peony season
HEIGHT 40 inches (102 cm)
SUPPORT Not needed
NOTE Named "Autumn" for the color tones. The cultivar's initials (A. H.) honor the pollen-parent, 'Alice Harding'.

'Banquet'

Arthur P. Saunders, 1941
UNITED STATES

Bright strawberry-red blooms with ruffled petals and dark center flares highlight the stamens. A feast for the eyes. Cut-leaf foliage is attractive in the garden all summer long.

KIND Lutea hybrid
COLOR Strawberry red
FLORAL FORM Semidouble
FRAGRANCE None
SEASON Mid tree peony season
HEIGHT 4 feet (1.2 m)
SUPPORT Not needed

'Baron Thyssen-Bornemisza'

Sir Peter Smithers, 1992
SWITZERLAND

Crinolines in mass, and with bountiful pink color tones, describe this frilly bloom. Purple flares draw your eye to the center of the large flower. Strong stems and abundant flowers up to 10 inches (25 cm) in size are wonderful attributes in the garden and for the vase.

KIND Suffruticosa group–rockii hybrid

COLOR Mauve pink with dark flares

FLORAL FORM Semidouble

FRAGRANCE Not noted

SEASON Mid tree peony season

HEIGHT To 5 feet (1.5 m) or taller

SUPPORT Not needed

CUT FLOWER Wonderful

NOTE The name honors one of central Europe's important industrialists and art collectors.

'Black Panther'

Arthur P. Saunders, 1948
UNITED STATES

Glossy, almost black-red petals are poised around the center of golden anthers, intense and riveting, as if something is about to pounce. Flowers are held above lacy foliage that adds distinction in the garden all summer long. The color has been compared to ripe Bing cherries, but this is more saturated towards black.

KIND Lutea hybrid

COLOR Maroon

FLORAL FORM Semidouble

FRAGRANCE Fragrant

SEASON Mid tree peony season

HEIGHT 4 feet (1.2 m)

SUPPORT Not needed

NOTE One of David's favorite peonies. Even passers-by slow down to stare.

'Boreas'

Nassos Daphnis, 1977
UNITED STATES

Petals are a very dark, rich burgundy and appear tousled by the wind. A fast-growing, tall specimen with deep green foliage.

KIND Lutea hybrid

COLOR Dark red

FLORAL FORM Semidouble

FRAGRANCE Not noted

SEASON Mid tree peony season

HEIGHT 4 feet (1.2 m)

SUPPORT Not needed

NOTE Appropriately named for the Greek god of the north winds.

AWARDS APS Best in Show 2013

'Brassy Lady'

William Seidl, 1996
UNITED STATES

Petal-packed, amber-tan flowers are stunningly attractive and show just above the foliage. Vigorous plants. Foliage has bronze undertones when young and turns deep green later.

KIND Lutea hybrid
COLOR Amber with overtones of tan, rose, and yellow
FLORAL FORM Double
FRAGRANCE Fragrant
SEASON Mid tree peony season
HEIGHT 36 inches (91 cm)
SUPPORT Not needed

'Brocaded Gown'

Toichi Domoto / Roy G. Klehm, after 1986
UNITED STATES

Dressed for the ball, blooms are ruffled crepepaper-pink, with a darker pink center and even darker pink flares. It's almost unreal and a very desirable beauty. Excellent foliage and vigor.

KIND Suffruticosa group
COLOR Pink
FLORAL FORM Semidouble
FRAGRANCE Fragrant
SEASON Early tree peony season
HEIGHT 36 inches (91 cm)
SUPPORT Not needed

'Dojean'

Sir Peter Smithers, 1990
SWITZERLAND

Elegance personified. The purity of the white petals is accented by deep and well-defined red flares. The *P. rockii* parentage contributes to the precise flares and to the plant's cold hardiness. A vigorous plant with healthy foliage.

KIND Suffruticosa group–rockii hybrid
COLOR White with red flares
FLORAL FORM Semidouble
FRAGRANCE None
SEASON Early tree peony season
HEIGHT 7 feet (2.1 m)
SUPPORT Not needed
NOTE Named for Lady Dojean, the wife of Sir Peter Smithers.

'Door County Sunset'

William Seidl, 1996
UNITED STATES

Summer sunset colors blended as in nature! Creamy-rose single flowers have a picotee edging and darker flares. Noted for blooming well, even after cold Wisconsin winters. This variety grows quickly and produces a spreading but fairly short plant.

KIND Lutea hybrid
COLOR Complex, creamy rose
FLORAL FORM Single
FRAGRANCE None
SEASON Mid tree peony season
HEIGHT 36 inches (91 cm)
SUPPORT Not needed
NOTE Named for the sunsets over Green Bay, as seen from Door County Peninsula of Wisconsin.

'Ezra Pound'

William Gratwick, 1986
UNITED STATES

Handsome, yet delicate flowers open light pink and fade to white as they mature. Dark-purple flares strongly accent the center. One is drawn in, as with Pound's poetry. A strong grower and large shrub.

KIND Suffruticosa group–rockii hybrid

COLOR Pale pink

FLORAL FORM Single to semidouble

FRAGRANCE Not noted

SEASON Early to mid tree peony season

HEIGHT 5 feet (1.5 m)

SUPPORT Not needed

NOTE Named for Ezra Pound, a brilliant and complex American poet.

'Fuchsia Ruffles'

William Seidl, 1996
UNITED STATES

Huge, frilly blooms of outstanding sensational color. Abundantly produced flowers are held nicely above the attractive foliage, which adds to their allure and visibility. A slow-growing plant and hardy in cold climates.

KIND Lutea hybrid

COLOR Fuchsia to reddish purple

FLORAL FORM Semidouble to double

FRAGRANCE Fragrant

SEASON Mid tree peony season

HEIGHT 34 inches (86 cm)

SUPPORT Not needed

'Gauguin'

Nassos Daphnis, before 1980
UNITED STATES

An artist's mix of strawberry red with yellow undertones, creating excitingly different shades each day, and from flower to flower. Ah, to spend a day in meditation viewing these! Good mounding green foliage backs the flowers well and works all summer long.

KIND Lutea hybrid

COLOR Strawberry red, with complex other tones

FLORAL FORM Single

FRAGRANCE Not noted

SEASON Mid tree peony season

HEIGHT To 4 feet (1.2 m)

SUPPORT Not needed

NOTE Clearly named for the vivid color palette confidently used by Paul Gauguin. Doubtless the painter would be more than honored.

'Godaishu'

before 1940
JAPAN

Elegant presentation of a multitude of purest-white orbs that open to softly fluffed blooms. An ancient Japanese variety. The flowers face the visitor atop vigorous shrubs.

KIND Suffruticosa group

COLOR White, with no flares

FLORAL FORM Semidouble

FRAGRANCE None

SEASON Mid tree peony season

HEIGHT 3 feet (91 cm)

SUPPORT Not needed

NOTE The name alludes to the large globe-shaped form and is most apt.

'Guardian of the Monastery'

William Gratwick, 1959
UNITED STATES

Large, strikingly colored, lavender to mauve flowers with deep-purple flares are a showstopper. Subtle color gradations across the petals are highlighted by the central boss of anthers that is held on lavender bases; bold, yet elegant. Shrubs benefit from some pruning after flowering, or they may become irregularly shaped over time, which itself can be a desired look.

KIND Suffruticosa group–rockii hybrid

COLOR Lavender

FLORAL FORM Semidouble

FRAGRANCE Slightly fragrant

SEASON Mid tree peony season

HEIGHT 4 feet (1.2 m)

SUPPORT Not needed

NOTE A classic American tree peony since it was raised by Gratwick before 1960. This was David's first tree peony, and the long-established shrub remains in a prime spot, where it always gets rave reviews from passers-by.

'Hana Kisoi'

before 1910
JAPAN

Large creped-pink flowers put on a stunning show. As flowers mature, the color is more strongly retained in the center, leading to a sublime floral display across the entire plant. Considered by many to be one of the finest classic pink tree peonies. Has been listed as 'Floral Rivalry'.

KIND Suffruticosa group

COLOR Pink

FLORAL FORM Semidouble to double

FRAGRANCE Fragrant

SEASON Early tree peony season

HEIGHT To 3 feet (91 cm)

SUPPORT Not needed

'Hephestos'

Nassos Daphnis, 1977
UNITED STATES

Vibrant, dark-red flowers exude power, both in color and flower form. Arresting attention, abundant large blooms are held high on the plant for our enjoyment. Good grower. Excellent and rewarding choice for gardeners just beginning to explore tree peonies.

KIND Lutea hybrid

COLOR Deep red

FLORAL FORM Double

FRAGRANCE Fragrant

SEASON Mid tree peony season

HEIGHT 4 feet (1.2 m)

SUPPORT Not needed

NOTE Named for the Greek god of fire.

AWARDS APS Gold Medal 2009; APS Best in Show 2012

'High Noon'

Arthur P. Saunders, 1952
UNITED STATES

Call it lemon yellow, butter yellow, or clear yellow, but just plant it in your garden if you've ever desired a yellow tree peony. The robust, semidouble flowers have raspberry-red flares at the base of the petals. Fragrance tends to citrus notes. Late-summer blooms sometimes appear, much to the delight of all. A vigorous tree peony, both for winter hardiness and height.

KIND Lutea hybrid

COLOR Yellow

FLORAL FORM Semidouble

FRAGRANCE Fragrant

SEASON Mid tree peony season

HEIGHT 4 feet (1.2 m), can grow to 5 feet (1.5 m)

SUPPORT Not needed

NOTE One of Saunders's yellows in his Golden Hind Group, 'High Noon' remains internationally popular for its clear color, fragrance, and occasional rebloom in late summer.

AWARDS APS Gold Medal 1989; APS Best in Show 1987; RHS Award of Garden Merit 2012

'Iphigenia'

Nassos Daphnis, 1977
UNITED STATES

Dramatic in its clear red color set off by dark flares and the light yellow of the central anthers, 'Iphigenia' has plentiful blooms on sturdy stems. A distinctive floral color on a hardy, mounded plant.

KIND Lutea hybrid

COLOR Red to maroon

FLORAL FORM Single to semidouble

FRAGRANCE Fragrant

SEASON Mid tree peony season

HEIGHT Up to 5 feet (1.5 m)

SUPPORT Not needed

NOTE At the beginning of the Trojan War, the gods ordered King Agamemnon to sacrifice his beloved daughter, Iphigenia, for his prayer to be heard. An epic and consequential decision of love versus power.

'Lavender Hill'

William Seidl, 1996
UNITED STATES

A grand show of abundant, large lavender blooms carried well on the surface of the entire bush! The graceful leaves are a pleasing backdrop, helping set off the intense purple flares of the excitingly colored flowers. The *P. rockii* parentage contributes cold hardiness.

KIND Suffruticosa group–rockii hybrid

COLOR Lavender

FLORAL FORM Semidouble with dark purple flares

FRAGRANCE Fragrant

SEASON Early tree peony season

HEIGHT 3 feet (91 cm)

SUPPORT Not needed

'Leda'

Nassos Daphnis, 1977
UNITED STATES

Gorgeous, intensely toned, mauve-pink petals are highlighted by deep plum-colored flares. The color gradations draw you in, almost with an air of mystery. Vigorous plants.

KIND Lutea hybrid

COLOR Pink

FLORAL FORM Semidouble

FRAGRANCE Slightly fragrant

SEASON Mid tree peony season

HEIGHT To 4 feet (1.2 m)

SUPPORT Not needed

NOTE Named for the Queen of Sparta and mother of Helen, whose beauty caused the Trojan War.

AWARDS APS Gold Medal 2014

'Marie Laurencin'

Nassos Daphnis, year not listed
UNITED STATES

Delightfully wavy shell-pink petals shade to deep rose at the center. A beautifully formed flower on a short plant.

KIND Lutea hybrid

COLOR Pink

FLORAL FORM Single to semidouble

FRAGRANCE None

SEASON Mid tree peony season

HEIGHT 30 inches (76 cm)

SUPPORT Not needed

NOTE Named after the French painter whose work before and after the First World War is now internationally respected.

'Mystic Mood'

William Seidl, 1996
UNITED STATES

A combination of complex neon color tones with simplicity of floral form makes for an outstanding garden specimen—a rising diva in the peony realm. Blooms are on long stems that reach out for your enjoyment, enhanced by the attractive foliage. Being from Wisconsin, this variety takes cold winters well.

KIND Lutea hybrid

COLOR Purple-lavender blend

FLORAL FORM Single

FRAGRANCE Fragrant

SEASON Mid tree peony season

HEIGHT To 4 feet (1.2 m)

SUPPORT Not needed

'Ofuji-nishiki'

before 1995
JAPAN

Simply ethereal! The Japanese combination of relatively simple floral form with sensational lavender tones, purple flares, and a golden center is soothing and harmonious. The lightly fragrant blooms are held in striking poses on a vigorously upright plant.

KIND Suffruticosa group

COLOR Lavender with dark purple flares

FLORAL FORM Semidouble

FRAGRANCE Slightly fragrant

SEASON Mid tree peony season

HEIGHT To 5 feet (1.5 m)

SUPPORT Not needed

NOTE The dark flares indicate there is *P. rockii* in the parentage of this stunning beauty. That parentage also contributes good winter hardiness.

'Pluto'

Nassos Daphnis, 1987
UNITED STATES

Vigorous shrub provides strong stems that hold the large, bold, ruffled, dark red blooms. The central boss of golden-yellow anthers almost glows in contrast.

KIND Lutea hybrid
COLOR Red
FLORAL FORM Semidouble
FRAGRANCE Fragrant
SEASON Mid tree peony season
HEIGHT 5 (1.5 m)
SUPPORT Not needed
NOTE Named for the Greek god of the underworld and considered one of Daphnis's finest dark reds.

'Princess Chiffon'

Toichi Domoto / Roy G. Klehm, 1987
UNITED STATES

Perhaps this should be the Princess of Chiffon. Either way, she's a large, cheerful bloom of crinkle-textured, vivid pink colors that lighten with age. Often one bud per stem.

KIND Suffruticosa group
COLOR Pink
FLORAL FORM Semidouble
FRAGRANCE Fragrant
SEASON Early tree peony season
HEIGHT 3 feet (91 cm)
SUPPORT Not needed

'Renown'

Arthur P. Saunders, 1949
UNITED STATES

Copper-red flowers of great simplicity on a lovely landscape
shrub. Occasionally reblooms. If this is your color range, there
is little like it. Capable of summer rebloom.

KIND Lutea hybrid

COLOR Red

FLORAL FORM Single

FRAGRANCE None

SEASON Mid tree peony season

HEIGHT 34 inches (86 cm)

SUPPORT Not needed

'Ruffled Sunset'

David L. Reath, 1988
UNITED STATES

A very appealing blend of rose pinks accented with darker center flares. Excellent amount of bloom. Flowers face outward, especially at the top of the shrub.

KIND Lutea hybrid

COLOR Rose pink

FLORAL FORM Single

FRAGRANCE Fragrant

SEASON Mid tree peony season

HEIGHT 3 feet (91 cm)

SUPPORT Not needed

AWARDS APS Best in Show 1991

'Shima-nishiki'

1951
JAPAN

A sensational floral riot. Each flower will be slightly different. Young plants may display solid red flowers, sometimes a white flower, but mostly they have red-and-white striping, especially as the plant matures. Definitely a tree peony for the bold of heart.

KIND Suffruticosa group

COLOR Red and white

FLORAL FORM Semidouble

FRAGRANCE None

SEASON Mid tree peony season

HEIGHT 4 feet (1.2 m)

SUPPORT Not needed

NOTE The name means "fire-flame" in Japanese. This is a white-variegated mutation of the red-flowered 'Taiyo', which is infrequently seen in North American gardens.

'Shintenchi'

before 1931
JAPAN

Large, ruffled, satiny, pink blooms can be up to 10 inches (25 cm) across. Prominent flares accent the petal bases. Imperially elegant.

KIND Suffruticosa group

COLOR Pink

FLORAL FORM Semidouble to double

FRAGRANCE None

SEASON Mid tree peony season

HEIGHT 4 feet (1.2 m)

SUPPORT Not needed

NOTE This is the first peony bred outside North America to receive the APS Gold Medal. As to the Japanese name, John C. Wister listed this as "New Heaven and Earth" in 1955.

AWARDS APS Gold Medal 1994

'Souvenir du Professor Maxime Cornu'

Louis Henry, 1907
FRANCE

Orange tones pop from the combination of yellow and deep pink. Huge blooms may be slightly pendant and seem to hide in the garden. Bring them indoors, where they glow when floated in a shallow bowl of water on a table and perfume the room. Sensational!

KIND Lutea hybrid
COLOR Complex yellows and pinks with orange tones
FLORAL FORM Double
FRAGRANCE Fragrant
SEASON Mid tree peony season
HEIGHT To 4 feet (1.2 m)
SUPPORT Not needed

CUT FLOWER Wonderful
NOTE Professor Maxime Cornu was the chair of horticulture at the National Museum in Paris with a specialty in plant diseases; he helped save the French wine industry in the late nineteenth century. This stunningly beautiful peony is also known as 'Kinkaku', a reference to an ancient imperial palace in Japan.

'Teni'

before 1993
JAPAN

A chiffon evening gown is evoked by this elegantly frilled pastel bloom. The large blooms with their complex tonal shading are carried on the plant where they are easily enjoyed.

KIND Suffruticosa group
COLOR Soft pink, stronger in the center
FLORAL FORM Double
FRAGRANCE Not noted
SEASON Early tree peony season
HEIGHT To 4 feet (1.2 m)
SUPPORT Not needed

'Theresa Anne'

William Seidl / Nathan Bremmer, 2013
UNITED STATES

Ruffled petals of cream and pink surround dark flares, accented by a profusion of yellow anthers at the center. An exuberance of blooms is presented on a relatively short and mounded tree peony.

KIND Lutea hybrid
COLOR Pink to rose with amber tones
FLORAL FORM Double
FRAGRANCE Not significant
SEASON Mid tree peony season
HEIGHT To 4 feet (1.2 m)
SUPPORT Not needed
NOTE The complex parentage of this stunning beauty combines many beloved tree peonies. This is one of the new Advanced Generation Lutea Hybrids.

'Toichi Ruby'

Toichi Domoto, 1986
UNITED STATES

A glowing ruby surely describes this floral jewel. The huge and beautiful flowers are held nicely above the foliage of the appealing shrub.

KIND Suffruticosa group
COLOR Red
FLORAL FORM Double
FRAGRANCE Fragrant
SEASON Mid tree peony season
HEIGHT 4 feet (1.2 m)
SUPPORT Not needed

'Vesuvian'

Arthur P. Saunders, 1948
UNITED STATES

An eruption of volcanic red flowers. Double, dark-red flowers cover the rounded shrub with abundant blooms. Each flower is not large, but individually and together, they are very attractive. The foliage makes a very nice and tidy landscape plant.

KIND Lutea hybrid
COLOR Dark red
FLORAL FORM Double
FRAGRANCE Lightly fragrant
SEASON Mid tree peony season
HEIGHT 25 inches (64 cm)
SUPPORT Not needed
NOTE Named for Mount Vesuvius, the legendary volcano near Naples, Italy.

'Waucedah Princess'

David L. Reath, 1988
UNITED STATES

Dark, central, lavender-red flares in this very symmetrical, lavender-pink flower add to its lustrous presence. Opens glistening pink, fades to a pale, elegant pink. Flowers well, even on relatively young plants, which have a mounding habit and pale green foliage.

KIND Lutea hybrid

COLOR Pink

FLORAL FORM Semidouble to double

FRAGRANCE Fragrant

SEASON Mid tree peony season

HEIGHT 26 inches (66 cm)

SUPPORT Not needed

NOTE Named for the local township near Reath's nursery in Michigan, likely meaning "in the pines."

'Yachiyo-tsubaki'

year not listed
JAPAN

A multitude of vivid coral-pink petals surround a central glowing sunshine-yellow boss of anthers—the effect is stunningly elegant. The color tones of the semidouble flowers are echoed in the slightly red-tinged foliage. Highly desired for its floral performance and longevity.

KIND Suffruticosa group

COLOR Coral pink

FLORAL FORM Semidouble

FRAGRANCE Not noted

SEASON Mid tree peony season

HEIGHT To 4 feet (1.2 m)

SUPPORT Not needed

NOTE Has been previously known as 'Eternal Camellias' and 'Thousand-year Camellias'.

AWARDS APS Best in Show 1979

'Zephyrus'

Nassos Daphnis, 1981
UNITED STATES

Opening pearlescent lavender, it matures to include pink and cream tones accented by dark flares nestled deep in the bloom. A relatively short tree peony with broad foliage.

KIND Lutea hybrid

COLOR Pink with complex creamy lavender tones and darker flares

FLORAL FORM Semidouble

FRAGRANCE Not noted

SEASON Mid tree peony season

HEIGHT To 4 feet (1.2 m)

SUPPORT Not needed

NOTE The Greek god of the west wind, a benevolent deity, is the namesake of this creamy-flowered beauty.

RESOURCES

Plant Sources

If you are interested in visiting a nursery, contact it in advance to see if they are able to invite you on the property. Web and mail-order nurseries without display grounds may have insurance or agricultural restrictions on nonstaff access.

CANADA

BRITISH COLUMBIA

Dutch Girl Peonies
5254 Queen Victoria Road
Beasley, BC V0G 2G2
www.peonyfarm.ca

Ferncliff Gardens
35344 McEwen Avenue
Mission, BC V2V 6R4
www.ferncliffgardens.com

Fraser's Thimble Farm
175 Arbutus Road
Salt Spring Island, BC V8K 1A3
www.thimblefarms.com

ONTARIO

Blossom Hill Nursery
681 Fife's Bay Road
Selwyn, ON K9J 6X4
www.blossomhillnursery.com

Peonies from the Field
2221 Bloor Street
Bowmanville, ON L1C 3K3
www.peoniesfromthefield.com

Peonygarden.com
2714 Highway #2
Jerseyville, ON L0R 1R0
www.peonygarden.com

QUÉBEC

Jardins Shefford
103 rue Clermont
Shefford, QC J2M 1X3
www.lesjardinsosiris.com

La Pivonerie D'Aoust
c.p. 220
Hudson Heights, QC J0P 1J0
www.paeonia.com

Les Jardins Osiris
818 rue Monique
St-Thomas de Joliette, QC J0K 3L0
www.lesjardinsosiris.com

Piviones Capano
566 route 138
Saint-Augustin-de-Desmaures, QC G3A 1W7
www.pivoinescapano.com

SASKATCHEWAN

Boreal Farms
RR #1, Site 10 Comp 8
Christopher Lake, QC S0J 0N0
www.borealfarms.net

UNITED KINGDOM

Bennison Peonies
East Firsby Grange
East Firsby
Market Rasen
Lincolnshire, England LN8 2DB
www.bennisonpeonies.co.uk

Binny Plants
Binny Estate
Ecclesmachan
West Lothian, Scotland EH52 6 NL
www.binnyplants.com

Cath's Garden Plants
The Walled Garden
Heaves Hotel
Heaves
Cumbria, England LA8 8EF
www.cathsgardenplants.co.uk

Claire Austin Hardy Plants
White Hopton Farm
Wern Lane, Sarn
Newtown, Wales SY16 4EN
www.claireaustin-hardyplants.co.uk

Cotswold Garden Flowers
Sands Lane
Badsey, Evesham
Worcestershire, England WR11 7EZ
www.cgf.net

Kelways Plants
Picts Hill
Langport
Somerset, England TA10 9EZ
www.kelways.co.uk

Perryhill Nurseries
Edenbridge Road
Hartfield
East Sussex, England TN7 4JP
www.perryhillnurseries.co.uk

Purely Peonies
8 Bourne Way
Addlestone
Surrey, England KT15 2BT
www.peonygrower.co.uk

Wisley Plant Centre
RHS Garden, Wisley
Woking
Surrey, England GU23 6QB
www.rhs.org.uk/gardens/wisley

Woodham Nursery
Eastbourne Road
South Godstone
Surrey, England RH9 8JB
www.woodhamnursery.co.uk

UNITED STATES

CALIFORNIA

Chateau CharMarron Peony Gardens
5335 Sierra Road
San Jose, CA 95132
www.4peonies.com

CONNECTICUT

Cricket Hill Garden
670 Walnut Hill Road
Thomaston, CT 06787
www.treepeony.com

ILLINOIS

Contrary Mary's Plants & Designs
2735 Route 52
Minooka, IL 60447
www.contrarymarysplants.com

KENTUCKY

Gold City Flower Gardens
6298 Gold City Road
Franklin, KY 42134
www.goldcityflowergardens.com

MASSACHUSETTS

Maple Ridge Peony Farm
1784 Main Poland Road
Conway, MA 01341
www.mapleridgepeonyfarm.com

MICHIGAN

Old House Gardens
536 Third Street
Ann Arbor, MI 48103
www.oldhousegardens.com

MINNESOTA

Aspelund Peony Gardens
9204 425th Street
Kenyon, MN 55946
www.aspelundpeonygardens.com

Countryside Gardens
10602 Fenner Avenue SE
Delano, MN 55328
www.growpeonies.com

Hidden Springs Flower Farm
18581 County Road 4
Spring Grove, MN 55974
www.hiddenspringsflowerfarm.com

Sevald Nursery
4937 Third Avenue South
Minneapolis, MN 55419
www.sevaldnursery.com

Swenson Gardens
P.O. Box 209
Howard Lake, MN 55349
www.swensongardens.com

MISSOURI

Gilbert H. Wild and Son
2944 State Highway 37
Reeds, Missouri 64859
www.gilberthwild.com

Hollingsworth Peonies
P.O. Box 233
Maryville, MO 64468
www.hollingsworthpeonies.com

NEW HAMPSHIRE

Birchwood Farms
45 LIttleworth Road
Dover, NH 03820
www.birchwoodfarmsnh.com

Peonies of the Coos Riviera
912 Connecticut River Road
Dalton, NH 03598
www.criv.com

NEW JERSEY

Peony's Envy
34 Autumn Hill Drive
Bernardsville, NJ 07924
www.peonysenvy.com

NEW YORK

Palmiter's Garden Nursery
2675 Avon Geneseo Road
Avon, NY 14414
www.palmitersgardennursery.com

OREGON

Adelman Peony Gardens
5690 Brooklake Road NE
Salem, OR 97305
www.peonyparadise.com

Brooks Gardens
6219 Topaz Street NE
Brooks, OR 97305
www.brooksgardens.com

VIRGINIA

André Viette Farm & Nursery
994 Long Meadow Road, Route 608
Fishersville, VA 22939
www.inthegardenradio.com

Roots & Blooms
500 Pantela Drive
Richmond, VA 23235
www.rootsandblooms.us

WASHINGTON

A & D Nursery
P.O. Box 2338
Snohomish, WA 98291
www.adpeonies.com

Peony Farm
2204 Happy Valley Road
Sequim, WA 98382
www.ilovepeonies.com

Pure Peonies
2949 East Badger Road
Everson, WA 98274
www.purepeonies.com

WISCONSIN

Fina Gardens
1319 8th Avenue
Hillsdale, WI 5473
www.finagardenspeonies.com

Klehm's Song Sparrow Farm & Nursery
13101 East Rye Road
Avalon, WI 53505
www.songsparrow.com

Oh My Peonies
W12925 Mielke Road
Marion, WI 54950
www.ohmypeonies.com

Solaris Farms
7510 Pinesva Road
Reedsville, WI 54230
www.solarisfarms.com

Cut Flower Sources

To find a local peony grower near you, contact the Association of Specialty Cut Flower Growers at www.ascfg.org.

CANADA

Piviones Capano
566 Route 138
Saint-Augustin-de-Desmaures, QC G3A 1W7
www.pivoinescapano.com

UNITED KINGDOM

English Peonies
Norfolk
England
www.englishpeonies.co.uk

UNITED STATES

ALASKA

Alaska Perfect Peonies
Box 15226, 55640 East Road
Fitz Creek, AK 99603
www.alaskaperfectpeony.com

Arctic Alaska Peonies
P.O. Box 74851
Fairbanks, AK 99707
www.arcticalaskapeonies.com

Polar Peonies
P.O. Box 84049
Fairbank, AK 99708
www.polarpeonies.com

MICHIGAN

Bridgewater Gardens
Saline, MI 48176
www.bridgewatergardens.com

NEW JERSEY

Sunset Flower Farm
550 Hands Mill Road
Belleplain, NJ 08270
www.sunsetflowerfarm.com

OREGON

Flyboy Naturals
15550 Old Highway 99 South
Myrtle Creek, OR 97457
www.flyboynaturals.com

Hammelmans Dried Floral
14477 Dominic Road NE
Mount Angel, OR 97362
www.hammelmans.com

WASHINGTON

Adeline's Peonies
502 Asotin Avenue
Toppenish, WA 98948
www.adelinespeonies.com

Pure Peonies
2949 East Badger Road
Everson, WA 98247
www.purepeonies.com

Public Gardens

Public gardens in Canada and the United States that are dedicated to conserving the diversity of horticultural and wild peonies as well as their public enjoyment are developing a peony consortium in the Plant Collections Network of the American Public Garden Association (https://publicgardens.org/programs/about-plant-collections-network).

CANADA

ALBERTA

Devonian Botanic Garden
University of Alberta
51227 AB-60
Parkland County, AB T7Y 1C5
https://devonian.ualberta.ca

Reader Rock Gardens
325 25 Avenue SE
Calgary, AB T2G 5V1
www.readerrock.com

BRITISH COLUMBIA

VanDusen Botanical Garden
5251 Oak Street
Vancouver, BC V6M 4H1
vandusengarden.org

NEW BRUNSWICK

Kingsbrae Garden
220 King Street
Saint Andrews, NB E5B 1Y8
www.kingsbraegarden.com

ONTARIO

Central Experimental Farm
Dominion Arboretum and Ornamental Gardens
Prince of Wales Drive
Ottawa, ON K1A 0C6
www.friendsofthefarm.ca

Oshawa Valley Botanical Gardens
155 Arena St
Oshawa, ON L1J 4E8
www.oshawa.ca/ovbg

Royal Botanical Gardens
680 Plains Road West
Burlington, ON L7T 4H4
www.rbg.ca

Whistling Gardens
698 Concession 3 Townsend Road
Wilsonville, ON N0E 1Z0
www.whistlinggardens.ca

QUÉBEC

Montréal Botanical Garden
4101 rue Sherbrooke E
Montréal, QC H1X 2B2
http://espacepourlavie.ca/en/botanical-garden

Reford Gardens
200 route 132
Grand-Métis, QC G0J 1Z0
www.refordgardens.com

IRELAND

National Botanic Gardens
Botanic Road
Glasnevin, Dublin 9
www.botanicgardens.ie

UNITED KINGDOM

Royal Botanic Garden Edinburgh
Arboretum Place
Edinburgh, Scotland EH3 5NZ
www.rbge.org.uk

Royal Botanic Gardens Kew
Kew, Richmond
Surrey, England TW9 3AB
www.kew.org

UNITED STATES

ALABAMA

Huntsville Botanical Garden
4747 Bob Wallace Avenue SW
Huntsville, AL 35805
www.hsvbg.org

ALASKA

Alaska Botanical Garden
4601 Campbell Airstrip Road
Anchorage, AK 99507
www.alaskabg.org

Georgeson Botanical Garden
University of Alaska Fairbanks
117 West Tanana Drive
Fairbanks, AK 99775
www.georgesonbotanicalgarden.org

Jenson-Olson Arboretum
23035 Glacier Highway
Juneau, AK 99801
www.juneau.org/parkrec/arboretum-main.php

CALIFORNIA

Filoli
86 Canada Road
Woodside, CA 94062
www.filoli.org

Japanese Tea Garden
75 Hagiwara Tea Garden Drive
San Francisco, CA 94118
www.japaneseteagardensf.com

San Francisco Botanical Garden
1199 9th Avenue
San Francisco, CA 94122
www.sfbotanicalgarden.org

The Huntington Library, Art Collections, and
Botanical Gardens
1151 Oxford Road
San Marino, CA 91108
www.huntington.org

COLORADO

Betty Ford Alpine Gardens
530 South Frontage Road East
Vail, CO 81657
www.bettyfordalpinegardens.org

Denver Botanic Gardens
1007 York Street
Denver, CO 80206
www.botanicgardens.org

CONNECTICUT

Philip Johnson Glass House
199 Elm Street
New Canaan, CT 06840
www.theglasshouse.org

DELAWARE

Winterthur Museum, Garden, and Library
5105 Kennett Pike
Winterthur, DE 19735
www.winterthur.org

DISTRICT OF COLUMBIA

United States National Arboretum
3501 New York Avenue NE
Washington, DC 20002
www.usna.usda.gov

IDAHO

Idaho Botanical Garden
2355 Old Penitentiary Road
Boise, ID 83712
www.idahobotanicalgarden.org

ILLINOIS

Allerton Park and Retreat Center
University of Illinois Urbana-Champaign
515 Old Timber Road
Monticello, IL 61856
www.allerton.illinois.edu

Chicago Botanic Garden
1000 Lake Cook Road
Glencoe, IL 60022
www.chicagobotanic.org

Klehm Arboretum and Botanic Garden
2715 South Main Street
Rockford, IL 61102
www.klehm.org

INDIANA

Benjamin Harrison Presidential Site
1230 North Delaware Street
Indianapolis, IN 46202
www.presidentbenjaminharrison.org/visit/gardens

IOWA

Bickelhaupt Arboretum
340 South 14th Street
Clinton, IA 52732
www.eicc.edu/about-eicc/
colleges-and-centers/bickelhaupt/

Dubuque Arboretum and Botanical Gardens
3800 Arboretum Drive
Dubuque, IA 52001
www.dubuquearboretum.com

Iowa Arboretum
1875 Peach Avenue
Madrid, IA 50156
www.iowaarboretum.org

Reiman Gardens
Iowa State University
1407 University Blvd
Ames, IA 50011
www.reimangardens.com

KANSAS

Botanica Wichita
701 Amidon Street
Wichita, KS 67203
www.botanica.org

Kansas State University Gardens
1500 Denison Avenue
Manhattan, KS 66506
www.k-state.edu/gardens

Overland Park Arboretum and Botanical Gardens
8909 West 179th Street
Overland Park, KS 66013
www.visitoverlandpark.com

KENTUCKY

Ashland, The Henry Clay Estate
120 Sycamore Road
Lexington, KY 40502
https://henry.org

Bernheim Arboretum
2499 Clermont Road
Clermont, KY 40110
www.bernheim.org

Cave Hill Cemetery Botanical Garden
701 Baxter Avenue
Louisville, KY 40204
www.cavehillheritagefoundation.org

Cherokee Park
745 Cochran Hill Road
Louisville, KY 40206
www.olmstedparks.org/our-parks/cherokee-park

Louisville Zoological Garden
1100 Trevilian Way
Louisville, KY 40213
https://louisvillezoo.org

Waterfront Botanical Gardens
129 East River Road
Louisville, KY 40202
www.waterfrontgardens.org

Whitehall Mansion and Gardens
3110 Lexington Road
Louisville, KY 40206
www.historicwhitehall.org/specimen-garden

Yew Dell Botanical Gardens
6220 Old LaGrange Road
Crestwood, KY 40014
www.yewdellgardens.org

MAINE

Gilsland Farm Audubon Center
20 Gilsland Farm Road
Falmouth, ME 04105
www.maineaudubon.org/find-us/gilsland-farm

MARYLAND

Belmont Manor and Historic Park
6555 Belmont Woods Road
Elkridge, MD 21075
www.belmontmanormd.com

MASSACHUSETTS

Arnold Arboretum
Harvard University
125 Arborway
Boston, MA 02130
www.arboretum.harvard.edu

The Botanic Garden of Smith College
16 College Lane
Northampton, MA 01063
www.smith.edu/garden

MICHIGAN

Peony Garden
Nichols Arboretum
University of Michigan
1610 Washington Heights
Ann Arbor, MI 48104
www.peony.mbgna.umich.edu

MINNESOTA

Arneson Acres Park
4711 West 70th Street
Edina, MN 55435
www.edinamn.gov/index.php?section=arneson-acres

Duluth Peony Gardens
Leif Erikson Park
12th Avenue East & London Road
Duluth, MN 55802
www.nycgovparks.org/parks/leif-ercisonp-parl

Lins Peony Garden
Lions Park
Lake Street West
Cologne, MN 55322
www.colognelions.com/lions-park

Minnesota Landscape Arboretum
3675 Arboretum
Chaska, MN 55318
www.arboretum.umn.edu

MISSOURI

The Ewing and Muriel Kauffman Memorial Garden
Powell Gardens
4800 Rockhill Road
Kansas City, MO 64110
www.powellgardens.org/
the-kauffman-memorial-garden

Linda Hall Library
University of Missouri-Kansas City
5109 Cherry Street
Kansas City, MO 64110
www.lindahall.org

Missouri Botanical Garden
4344 Shaw Blvd
St. Louis, MO 63110
www.missouribotanicalgarden.org

Springfield Botanical Gardens
2400 South Scenic Avenue
Springfield, MO 65807
www.parkboard.org/botanical

NEBRASKA

Lauritzen Gardens
Omaha's Botanical Center
100 Bancroft Street
Omaha, NE 68108
www.lauritzengardens.org

Sass Memorial Iris Garden
Eugene T. Mahoney State Park
28500 West Park Highway
Ashland, NE 68003
www.greateromahairissociety.org

NEW YORK

Brooklyn Botanic Garden
990 Washington Avenue
Brooklyn, NY 11225
www.bbg.org

Cornell Botanic Gardens
Cornell University
1 Plantations Road
Ithaca, NY 14850
www.cornellbotanicgardens.org/
our-gardens/botanical

Grant Garden
Hamilton College Arboretum
198 College Hill Road
Clinton, NY 13323
www.hamilton.edu/arboretum/home

Linwood Gardens
1912 York Road West
Pavilion, NY 14525
www.linwoodgardens.org

New York Botanical Garden
Dolores DeFina Hope Tree Peony Collection
2900 Southern Boulevard
Bronx, NY 10458
www.nybg.org

Rockefeller State Park Preserve
125 Phelps Way
Pleasantville, NY 10570
https://parks.ny.gov/parks/59/details.aspx

Shacksboro Schoolhouse Museum
46 Canton Street
Baldwinsville, NY 13027
www.shacksboromuseum.com

Snug Harbor Cultural Center
and Botanical Garden
1000 Richmond Terrace
Staten Island, NY 10301
www.snug-harbor.org

NORTH CAROLINA

JC Raulston Arboretum
4415 Beryl Road
Raleigh, NC 27606
https://jcra.ncsu.edu

Sarah P. Duke Gardens
420 Anderson Street
Durham NC 27705
gardens.duke.edu

NORTH DAKOTA

Peony Garden
North Dakota Museum of Art
261 Centennial Drive
Grand Forks, ND 58202
www.ndmoa.com/peony-garden

OHIO

Kingwood Center Gardens
900 Park Avenue West
Mansfield, OH 44906
www.kingwoodcenter.org

OREGON

Lan Su Chinese Garden
239 NW Everett
Portland, OR 97209
www.lansugarden.org

The Oregon Garden
879 West Main Street
Silverton, OR 97381
www.oregongarden.org

PENNSYLVANIA

Barnes Arboretum
300 North Latch's Lane
Merion, PA 19066
www.barnesfoundation.org/visit/merion

Longwood Gardens
1001 Longwood Road
Kennett Square, PA 19348
www.longwoodgardens.org

Scott Arboretum of Swarthmore College
500 College Avenue
Swarthmore, PA 19081
www.scottarboretum.org

SOUTH DAKOTA

Mary Jo Wegner Arboretum
1900 South Perry Place
Sioux Falls, SD 57110
www.maryjowegnerarboretum.com

McCrory Gardens
South Dakota State University
631 22nd Avenue
Brookings, SD 57006
www.mccrorygardens.com

VERMONT

Hildene
The Lincoln Family Home
1005 Hildene Road
Manchester, VT 05254
www.hildene.org

Shelburne Museum
6000 Shelburne Road
Shelburne, VT 05482
https://shelburnemuseum.org

VIRGINIA

Meadowlark Botanical Gardens
9750 Meadowlark Gardens Court
Vienna, VA 22182
www.novaparks.com/parks/
meadowlark-botanical-gardens

Lewis Ginter Botanical Garden
1800 Lakeside Avenue
Henrico, VA 23228
www.lewisginter.org

WASHINGTON

Seattle Chinese Garden
6000 16th Avenue SW
Seattle, WA 98106
www.seattlechinesegardem.org

Washington Park Arboretum
2300 Arboretum Drive East
Seattle, WA 98112
https://botanicgardens.uw.edu/
washington-park-arboretum

WISCONSIN

Boerner Botanical Gardens
9400 Boerner Drive
Hales Corners, WI 53130
www.boernerbotanicalgardens.org

Hoard Historical Museum
401 Whitewater Avenue
Fort Atkinson, WI 53538
www.hoardmuseum.org

Olbrich Botanical Gardens
3330 Atwood Avenue
Madison, WI 53704
www.olbrich.org

Rotary Botanical Gardens
1455 Palmer Drive
Janesville, WI 53545
www.rotarybotanicalgardens.org

Sisson's Peony Gardens
221-291 North Main Street
Rosendale, WI 54974
www.rosendale.wlhn.org/peony.htm

USDA Hardiness Zones

Temp °F			Zone	Temp °C		
−60	to	−55	1A	−51	to	−48
−55	to	−50	1B	−48	to	−46
−50	to	−45	2A	−46	to	−43
−45	to	−40	2B	−43	to	−40
−40	to	−35	3A	−40	to	−37
−35	to	−30	3B	−37	to	−34
−30	to	−25	4A	−34	to	−32
−25	to	−20	4B	−32	to	−29
−20	to	−15	5A	−29	to	−26
−15	to	−10	5B	−26	to	−23
−10	to	−5	6A	−23	to	−21
−5	to	0	6B	−21	to	−18
0	to	5	7A	−18	to	−15
5	to	10	7B	−15	to	−12
10	to	15	8A	−12	to	−9
15	to	20	8B	−9	to	−7
20	to	25	9A	−7	to	−4
25	to	30	9B	−4	to	−1
30	to	35	10A	−1	to	2
35	to	40	10B	2	to	4
40	to	45	11A	4	to	7
45	to	50	11B	7	to	10
50	to	55	12A	10	to	13
55	to	60	12B	13	to	16
60	to	65	13A	16	to	18
65	to	70	13B	18	to	21

Find hardiness maps on the Internet.

UNITED STATES usna.usda.gov/Hardzone/ushzmap.html

CANADA planthardiness.gc.ca

EUROPE houzz.com/europeZoneFinder

FURTHER READING

In addition to the readings listed here, the American Peony Society has a series of publications.

Fearnley-Whittingstall, Jean. 1999. *Peonies*.
    New York: Abrams.

Halda, Josef J., and James W. Waddick. 2004. *The Genus* Paeonia.
    Portland, Oregon: Timber Press.

Harding, Alice. 1917. *The Book of the Peony*.
    Philadelphia and London: J. B. Lippincott Company.

Page, Martin. 2005. *The Gardener's Peony: Herbaceous and Tree Peonies*.
    Portland, Oregon: Timber Press.

Rogers, Allan. 1995. *Peonies*.
    Portland, Oregon: Timber Press.

Upjohn, William E. ca.1923. *Brook Lodge Gardens—Peonies*.
    Accessed at http://peony.mbgna.umich.edu/sites/default/files/files/BrookLodge.pdf.

Wister, John C., ed. 1962. *The Peonies*.
    Washington, D.C.: American Horticultural Society.

PHOTO CREDITS

All photos are by Carol A. Adelman unless otherwise stated here.

INDEX

ABOUT THE AUTHORS

photo by William Brinkerhoff

photo by Hannah Gustin

DAVID C. MICHENER is associate curator at the University of Michigan Matthaei Botanical Gardens and Nichols Arboretum in Ann Arbor, where he is overseeing the rejuvenation of the Peony Garden, the largest public collection of historic herbaceous peonies in North America. A popular speaker and co-author of *Taylor's Guide to Groundcovers*, David has visited over 500 gardens worldwide, often as leader of garden-study tours. In 2014 he was awarded a Professional Citation of Merit from the American Public Garden Association. His own garden encompasses scores of peonies and has appeared in several publications and been included in several garden tours. With colleagues at the Central Botanical Gardens in Belarus, especially Dr. Nastassia Vlasova, he is identifying herbaceous peony cultivars and deducing their unrecorded genetic ancestry at both institutions using DNA "fingerprinting." David earned a doctorate in botany from Claremont Graduate School in California.

CAROL A. ADELMAN and her husband own and operate Adelman Peony Gardens near Salem, Oregon, where they grow 484 varieties of peonies—bush, tree and Itoh peonies. Their garden is featured in *The Pacific Northwest Garden Tour* by Donald Olson. A popular speaker, Carol is also internationally respected for her knowledge of peonies. Since first exhibiting at the American Peony Society Show in 2002, she has placed in Court of Honor every year and received Grand Champion designation eight out of twelve years. She is on the Board of Directors for the American Peony Society and on the international Peony Advisory Board for the Peony Garden at Nichols Arboretum. She is President of the Pacific North West Peony Society, and Charter Organizer of the Salem Hardy Plant Society.